AF263978

BEST OF THE SNOWBIRDS
EXPAT RADIO PODCAST

CANADIANS HEADING SOUTH FOR THE WINTERS!

What you don't know will hurt you!

Gerald A Scott

Table of Contents

DISCLAIMER

This book is written by Gerry A. Scott in their individual capacity and not as a registered representation of Raymond James Ltd. (RJL) or any of its affiliates. It expresses the opinions of the authors and not necessarily those of RJL or any of its affiliates. This book is provided as a general source of information and should not be considered personal investment advice or financial planning advice. It should not be construed as an offer or solicitation for the sale or purchase of any product and should not be considered tax advice. We are not tax advisors and we recommend that clients seek independent advice from a professional advisor on tax-related matters. We recommend any individual seek independent advice from an investment advisor prior to making any investment decisions and from a professional accountant concerning tax-related matters. Statistics, factual data and other information are from sources RJL believes to be reliable, but their accuracy cannot be guaranteed. This book is furnished on the basis and understanding that RJL or any of its affiliates are to be under no liability whatsoever in respect therefore. This book may provide reference to third-party services. RJL or any of its affiliates is not responsible for the availability of these external services, nor does RJL or any of its affiliates endorse, warrant or guarantee the products, services or information described or offered. US-based securities-related products and services are offered through Raymond James (USA) Ltd., member FINRA/SIPC.

WHY THIS BOOK EXISTS

Many Canadians approach the Snowbird lifestyle with a simple assumption: follow familiar patterns, stay roughly under six months, and everything else will take care of itself. Advice circulates easily — from neighbours, long-time winter travelers, and well-meaning friends — and much of it sounds reasonable.

Thousands of Canadians have reached out to me over the years—through emails and calls—completely overwhelmed and anxious because they discovered the truth too late.

The difficulty is not that any one rule is unclear. The difficulty is that several independent systems evaluate the same behavior at the same time.

The realization became clear to me during what should have been an ordinary client review. A careful, organized individual had spent years wintering in the United States without incident. When I mapped his travel history against the IRS Substantial Presence Test, provincial health requirements, and Canadian tax residency rules, nothing appeared problematic in isolation. Each rule made sense on its own. The complication emerged only when those rules were applied together.

Around that same period, people close to me encountered similar surprises. One family friend was questioned at the border because his travel pattern resembled something more permanent than intended. Another discovered that her established winter routine placed her closer to U.S. tax residency than she realized. Neither situation arose from carelessness. Both stemmed from following informal guidance without understanding how multiple systems interpret the same facts.

Three systems consistently shape Snowbird life:

- U.S. immigration evaluates patterns, duration, and intent.

- The IRS analyzes cumulative day counts and income connections.

- Canadian authorities assess physical presence and ongoing residential ties.

For most Snowbirds, complications do not begin with dramatic decisions. They begin with ordinary ones — extending a stay, returning for a second trip, purchasing property, working remotely for a few weeks, or leaving assets behind. Individually, these choices feel routine. Collectively, they form a pattern that agencies evaluate differently than the traveler might expect.

Cross-border life is manageable. But it is manageable only when viewed as an interconnected structure rather than a series of separate rules.

How I Found My Way Into This Work

I did not begin my career expecting to work in the cross-border world. My parents were working people. My father repaired engines. My mother cleaned rooms in local resorts to help keep us steady. We learned early that effort mattered more than opportunity, and nothing in my upbringing suggested that I would one day build a professional life across two countries.

The town where I grew up was small enough that the boundaries felt familiar. Most people stayed, and their lives followed the rhythm of the place. I am grateful for that start. It taught me to value practicality, consistency, and responsibility. But curiosity pushed me outward.

Moving to Vancouver in my early twenties opened a new world. New expectations. New ways of thinking. Not long after settling in, I found my way into financial services. It was an immediate recognition — a field that matched the way my mind worked. A person's financial life is a map, and I became deeply interested in understanding how decisions connect over time.

As my work expanded, I obtained credentials to practice on both sides of the border. Clients were no longer simply saving or investing. Many were structuring their financial lives around extended time in the United States, managing retirement income, property ownership, and cross-border tax considerations related to seasonal living. The questions became more complex, and I wanted to answer them accurately.

My own life played a quiet role in that shift. My first trip to Maui in 1981 left an imprint, and over the years I spent more time in the United States. That experience required me to understand the rules for myself — immigration considerations, tax residency, tracking days, health coverage. Enjoying time abroad demanded clarity, not assumptions.

As I shared these insights, the questions grew. Clients wanted guidance tailored to their situations. Listeners and readers alike wanted clearer guidance on the parts of the system that seemed most uncertain. It became clear that people were not lacking discipline — they were lacking reliable information.

I did not plan to become a cross-border specialist. It happened gradually, shaped by the people who trusted me with their planning and by my own experience navigating two systems at once.

Currently, I have spent 35 years—and counting—in the wealth management world. Over the last decade, my work has focused almost entirely on the cross-border space. I hold portfolio management licences in both Canada and the United States, and I'm fully designated to write comprehensive financial plans for Canadians who spend part of the year in the United States, including Snowbirds and individuals navigating cross-border tax and residency considerations related to extended winter stays.

This book grows out of that work.

INTRODUCTION

Why start here? Because everything that follows depends on one simple truth:

If you spend part of your life in another country, the rules will shape your experience whether you understand them or not.

My aim is to help you navigate them with clarity rather than uncertainty.

Understanding The Real Cross-Border Challenge

For many Canadians, the Snowbird lifestyle begins as a reward. Retirement creates flexibility. Family spreads across borders. A warmer climate offers comfort. The decision to spend time in the United States feels personal and practical.

What few people anticipate is that cross-border living is not simply a change in location. It is the beginning of an ongoing legal and financial relationship with another country.

The real risk is not complexity — it is gradual exposure. It is the cumulative effect of repeated presence over time. Once winters in the United States become part of your routine, your travel patterns, income sources, property ownership, and residential ties begin to form a measurable profile. That profile carries consequences — even if each individual season feels routine.

A winter abroad may feel temporary. A decade of winters becomes an established cross-border footprint — one shaped by income streams, property ownership, reporting obligations, and healthcare eligibility that accumulate over time.

Many Snowbirds focus on the immediate year. They ask:

- How long can I stay?
- Do I need to file anything?
- Will my health card remain valid?

These are important questions, but they are short-term in nature. Long-term stability depends on something deeper: intentional structure. Cross-border living influences future tax treatment, estate planning, and asset structuring decisions. A strategy that works comfortably in the early years of retirement may create complications later if it evolves without deliberate oversight.

This book addresses those long-term considerations directly.

It explains how U.S. tax residency can arise from cumulative presence and how to prevent unintended classification. It clarifies when and how to file protective forms such as Form 8840. It outlines how Canadian residency is evaluated through primary and secondary ties, and why provincial healthcare thresholds matter more than many realize. It examines how property ownership in the United States can affect reporting and estate exposure. It discusses the risks associated with remote work while visiting.

The objective is not to limit mobility. It is to protect it.

Cross-border living offers opportunity and flexibility when it is managed with foresight. When it is approached casually, however, small structural misalignments can surface at moments when stability matters most — during retirement transitions, healthcare needs, property sales, or estate settlement.

The central theme throughout these chapters is sustainability. How do you enjoy time in another country without compromising your tax position? How do you preserve Canadian residency strength while spending meaningful time in the U.S.? How do you ensure that today's convenience does not become tomorrow's complication?

This book brings those questions into one coherent framework. It provides a method for evaluating your cross-border exposure before it evaluates you. By understanding how your decisions accumulate over time, you retain control over how your life is classified — and preserve the freedom that made the Snowbird lifestyle appealing in the first place.

That is the real cross-border challenge.

Tools That Help Make Sense Of A Complex System

As cross-border questions became more frequent, it became clear that explanation alone was not enough. People did not need more warnings; they needed structure. Managing overlapping rules requires consistent tracking, reliable calculations, and informed interpretation.

That need led to the development of practical tools designed to reduce uncertainty.

Snowbirds U.S. Day Tracker App

Built to calculate day counts using the IRS three-year formula, the app allows users to enter travel dates manually and view cumulative totals clearly. Its purpose is accuracy — not estimation — so individuals can make informed decisions before thresholds are reached.

Snowbirds Expat Radio Podcast

The podcast brings together immigration lawyers, accountants, tax specialists, financial planners, and other professionals whose perspectives help clarify complex cross-border questions. It provides context where numbers alone are not enough.

Together, these resources provide structure:

- The apps handle the calculations.

- The podcast provides professional insight.

Cross-border planning is not about eliminating complexity. It is about understanding it clearly enough to move through it with confidence.

Case Studies Throughout

You will find case studies woven into the chapters. They are drawn from years of client work and professional discussions. Each one shows how real people encounter problems, how those problems develop, and how clarity or the tracking tools helped them avoid more serious consequences.

How to Read This Book

You do not need to follow a linear path.

Some readers start with the chapter that speaks directly to their concerns. Others read from beginning to end. Both approaches work.

Each chapter stands on its own while contributing to a complete understanding of the cross-border landscape.

Use the structure as a map. Mark what applies today. Return to what may matter later. Treat the case studies and tools as practical guides rather than abstract explanations.

A Note Of Gratitude

I have learned over the years that no one builds a career like this alone. The work may be technical, and much of it is done quietly at a desk or in conversation with clients, but the steady support in the background is what makes it possible.

My family has been part of this journey from the beginning. Melissa has lived through every phase of my career, including the periods when I was trying to understand the cross-border space one rule at a time. Her patience, and the way she encourages me to keep moving toward clarity even when the material is demanding, has shaped more of this work than she realizes.

My daughter, Chelsea, has grown up with this world woven into family life. She has listened to ideas long before they were recorded for the podcast or written into planning documents. Her children, London, Harper, and Rhodes, bring a sense of perspective that always grounds me. They notice things in the simplest way. They see a podcast episode not as a technical discussion but as something their grandfather created. Their excitement reminds me why clarity matters. People deserve to understand their world without feeling overwhelmed.

Carson has also been part of this growth. He joined our wealth management firm years ago and helped strengthen the discipline and structure behind the work. His contribution has been practical and steady, and those qualities have influenced how we approach decisions, planning, and long-term strategy.

Over the course of my life, there have been many dogs as well. Lassie, Maggie, Teasha, Stewy, Lilly, Diesel, Albert, and Kilo each brought their own presence into our home. They were loyal in the uncomplicated way that only animals can be, and they added warmth to the years when my work was becoming increasingly demanding. They are part of our family history, and acknowledging them feels natural here.

I have also been fortunate to have friends and colleagues whose judgment I trust. They may not appear by name in this book, but their influence is present in the questions they asked, the discussions we had, and the experiences we shared along the way.

This project is not simply the result of professional experience. It is the product of a life supported by people who made room for the work, the learning, and the responsibility that came with it. For that, I am grateful.

Before We Begin

Cross-border planning is not something people pursue for its own sake. It grows out of a desire to live well, to enjoy the places that matter to you, and to make decisions without hesitation. If you understand the rules, that life becomes far easier to maintain. If you do not, the simplest moments can become complicated in ways no one expects.

My aim in the chapters ahead is straightforward. I want to give you a clear view of the landscape so you can move through it with confidence. The material is detailed, but it does not need to be confusing. With the right structure, the rules become manageable and the decisions more predictable.

Looking Ahead: The Next Chapter

Chapter One explains the foundational structure of cross-border living for Snowbirds. It addresses common misunderstandings, including the six-month myth, how the IRS counts days under the Substantial Presence Test, how CBP evaluates travel patterns and intent, and how Canadian residency is determined through primary and secondary ties. The chapter also introduces the "three-system" framework—immigration, U.S. tax, and Canadian residency—and shows how confusion arises when these systems are treated as one. This foundation prepares readers to approach the rest of the book with precision rather than assumption.

CHAPTER ONE
UNDERSTANDING THE FOUNDATIONS OF CROSS-BORDER LIVING

Why Snowbirds Misunderstand the Rules

Most people begin the Snowbird lifestyle with a simple intention: leave the winter behind, enjoy a few months of warmth, return home when the season changes. Nothing about that plan feels complicated. And because it feels uncomplicated, people assume the rules surrounding it are equally straightforward.

The misunderstandings rarely start with dramatic choices. They begin with confidence built from years of hearing the same familiar phrases.

"You get six months."
"Just don't work in the United States."
"If you're not earning money there, you're fine."
"Everyone does it this way."

These sayings circulate in communities, at golf courses, in winter parks, at coffee gatherings, and they become so common that they start to feel authoritative. But none of them describe the rules accurately. They describe *comfort*, not compliance. That is where most confusion begins.

Why people misread the system

Snowbirds do not misunderstand the rules because they are careless. They misunderstand them because the rules are divided across different agencies that do not explain how they fit together.

- **Immigration** cares about patterns and intent
- **The IRS** cares about cumulative presence and tax residency
- **Provincial health plans** care about maintaining ties to Canada

No one is responsible for giving Snowbirds a complete picture, and that absence creates space for half-truths to spread.

A pattern I have seen for decades

New Snowbirds often feel confident until the first moment something asks for precision. A border officer asks a few probing questions. A tax preparer requests exact dates. A travel insurance provider wants proof of presence in Canada. Suddenly, the casual approach that worked socially does not work administratively.

This is where most people realise the rules were more layered than they expected.

Key Idea

Snowbird mistakes rarely come from breaking rules.

They come from not knowing which rules apply.

Understanding that is the foundation of everything that follows in this chapter.

The Six-Month Myth and Why It Misleads People

The idea that Snowbirds are automatically entitled to six months in the United States is one of the most persistent beliefs in Canadian communities. It passes from neighbor to neighbor with a confidence that makes it sound official. Many people build their entire travel plan around it. Yet the statement has no grounding in law. It is a simplified approximation that fails the moment a real system tests it.

Where the myth comes from

The misunderstanding grows from a mix of casual observation and incomplete knowledge. Most Canadians know someone who routinely spends about six months away without incident. Those smooth experiences become the basis for a rule that does not exist. When repeated often enough, the story starts to overshadow the actual regulations.

What people believe

Most Snowbirds assume the following:

- Immigration grants every Canadian six months by default
- Staying under six months avoids tax connections
- Six months aligns with provincial health rules

None of these assumptions holds true.

What immigration actually sees

A U.S. Customs and Border Protection officer does not guarantee six months. The officer decides how long to admit a traveller based on:

- travel frequency
- duration of previous stays
- perceived ties to Canada
- any indication of work, residence, or intent to stay long term

If your pattern resembles residency rather than tourism, the officer can shorten the stay. Many Snowbirds discover this only after they have planned an entire season.

Why the myth is dangerous

The problem with believing in the six-month rule is not just that it is wrong — it is that it encourages people to ignore the other timelines they are obligated to track.

- The IRS does not use a six-month rule.
- Provincial health plans do not use a six-month rule.
- Tax residency definitions do not use a six-month rule.

Yet Snowbirds often treat "six months" as the only number that matters. When multiple systems evaluate your movements differently, relying on one simplified idea creates gaps no one notices until the consequences arrive.

Key Idea

The six-month myth is comfortable, familiar, and deeply misleading.

The real rules are more nuanced, and they do not agree with one another.

This is the first major misunderstanding most Snowbirds confront — and one of the most important to correct before moving deeper into cross-border planning.

How the IRS Actually Counts Days

Most Snowbirds first hear about the IRS Substantial Presence Test only after they have already created a pattern that the IRS would interpret as tax residency. By that point, the concern usually feels sudden and unexpected. The confusion comes from one simple fact: the IRS does not measure time the way most people think it does.

The IRS does not care about single-year totals

When Canadians talk about time in the United States, they think in calendar years.

"How many days was I there this year?"

The IRS uses a different lens. It looks at a three-year pattern and weighs the days differently. That structure often catches people off guard because it does not resemble any common-sense approach to counting.

How the formula works

The IRS applies this calculation:

- All days in the current year count fully
- One third of the days from the previous year count
- One sixth of the days from the year before that count

If the combined total reaches 183, the IRS treats you as a U.S. tax resident unless you take steps to claim a closer connection to Canada.

This test is mechanical. It does not evaluate intent, purpose of visit, or reason for travel. It evaluates presence.

Why this feels counterintuitive

A Snowbird may spend fewer than 183 days in any single year and still fail the IRS test because the prior years' visits contribute to the equation. Someone who spends between 120 and 150 days consistently each winter may move into tax residency territory without ever crossing what they believe to be the limit.

That pattern surprises people. They assume that staying below six months in a single year protects them. The IRS is not looking at one year. It is looking at the behavior over time.

Why this test matters

Tax residency has significant implications. It can require filing a U.S. tax return, reporting worldwide income, and establishing additional disclosure obligations. Most Snowbirds do not intend to become U.S. tax residents, and most are unaware that their long-term pattern may place them in that category.

Key Idea

IRS residency is not about what you intend.
It is about the pattern your days create.

Understanding this calculation is essential. Without it, Snowbirds plan their stays based on assumptions that do not match how the IRS interprets their behavior.

Immigration Patterns and How CBP Interprets Your Visits

Immigration rules are often misunderstood because they appear straightforward at the surface. Canadians enter the United States as visitors. Visitors are allowed to stay for a period of time. Most people assume that if they remain polite, truthful, and within what they believe to be the accepted timeframe, they will be admitted without difficulty.

But immigration decisions hinge on something less visible: **patterns**.

Immigration looks for behaviour, not calculations

Unlike the IRS, immigration does not use formulas or weighted timelines.

A U.S. Customs and Border Protection officer looks at your overall pattern of travel and asks a few practical questions:

- Does this person appear to be a visitor?
- Do their travel habits suggest a shift toward residence?
- Are they slowly building a life in the United States?

None of these questions is written into a chart. They are part of the officer's judgement, shaped by experience.

Signals that raise questions

Most Snowbirds do not intentionally raise concerns. The issues arise from ordinary life habits that slowly accumulate meaning.

CBP may question a traveler more closely if they notice:

- stays that grow longer each year
- a pattern of returning quickly after each departure

- possession of items that resemble household goods
- a vehicle left in the United States
- utilities or memberships tied to a U.S. address
- statements suggesting "wintering" rather than visiting

These are not violations on their own. They are indicators that your lifestyle may be shifting from tourism to residency.

Why intent matters

CBP officers are evaluating intent every time a visitor arrives. You may be entering for the winter, but if your pattern resembles relocation — especially if it includes remote work, extended stays, or practical ties to a U.S. property — the officer may shorten the admission period or ask more detailed questions.

Snowbirds who have never been questioned are often surprised when it happens for the first time. From their perspective, nothing has changed. From the officer's perspective, the accumulated pattern has shifted.

The tension between personal routine and immigration interpretation

Snowbirds often say, "But I have always done it this way."

CBP does not look at history the way travelers do.

A pattern that once appeared harmless can look different when it continues over multiple seasons.

Understanding how immigration interprets those patterns is essential to maintaining smooth entry.

Key Idea

Immigration decisions are based on judgement, not formulas. Your pattern tells a story — and CBP is trained to read it.

Maintaining Canadian Residency: What Authorities Actually Look For

Many Snowbirds assume that residency is defined by where they feel most connected or where they spend the majority of their time. In daily life, that interpretation makes sense. In the eyes of Canadian authorities, residency is determined by something more structured and considerably more specific.

Two areas matter most:
your ties to Canada and **your physical presence**.

Neither works alone. They reinforce each other.

What residency means in practical terms

Canadian residency is not established through a single document or action. It is demonstrated through a collection of ties that reflect where your life is anchored. These ties carry different weights depending on their nature. Some are considered primary and more influential; others support the overall picture.

Primary residential ties

Authorities look closely at:

- a home available to you in Canada
- a spouse or partner living in Canada
- dependents who reside in Canada

If these ties remain strong, your residency is supported even when you spend extended periods outside the country.

Secondary supporting ties

These details reinforce your connection:

- Canadian driver's license
- Canadian provincial health card
- active bank accounts
- ongoing club or community memberships
- personal belongings kept in Canada

Individually, they may seem minor. Together, they shape how your residency is interpreted.

Why these ties matter

Canadian tax residency determines:

- which country has primary claim over your worldwide income
- how your tax filings must be structured
- whether you remain eligible for provincial health coverage

People often believe that filing taxes or owning a home is enough. In reality, residency is assessed through a mosaic of ties, and authorities evaluate the entire picture.

The danger of weakening ties without noticing

Some Snowbirds unintentionally erode their residency profile over time.

Example patterns include:

- transferring most financial accounts to the United States
- selling or renting out their Canadian home without maintaining another
- spending more time abroad than in Canada
- allowing provincial health coverage to lapse
- gradually shifting their community involvement south

No single action determines residency. It is the cumulative effect that raises questions.

Key Idea

Residency is not about where you prefer to spend your time. It is about where your life remains anchored.

Understanding this distinction is essential before exploring the more technical aspects of tax, immigration, and long-term planning.

The Three-System Problem

A large part of Snowbird confusion comes from treating the rules as if they belong to a single framework. They do not. The cross-border world is shaped by three separate systems, each of which evaluates your behavior through its own criteria. Understanding this division is one of the most important steps in planning a stable Snowbird lifestyle.

1. Immigration rules

Immigration is concerned with the nature of your visits.
Its questions are practical:

- Are you a visitor?
- Do your patterns resemble residence?
- Are you maintaining ties to your home country?

These decisions are judgment-based. One officer may focus on frequency of travel. Another may look at belongings you bring. Another may question how long you stay each season.

Immigration does not consider your tax status or provincial health coverage.

2. IRS tax rules

The IRS evaluates presence, income, and the potential for tax residency.

It uses formulas, thresholds, and reporting requirements that operate independently of immigration decisions. The IRS does not take into account how long immigration allowed you to stay. It examines your cumulative days, income connections, and the pattern created by your travel history.

Many Snowbirds assume that if immigration permits a stay, the IRS must view it the same way. The two systems do not speak to each other.

3. Canadian residency and health rules

Canada focuses on the strength of your ties and your physical presence for tax and provincial health purposes.

These rules are meant to determine whether your life remains anchored in Canada, not whether you enjoy spending winters somewhere else. A Snowbird can be fully compliant with immigration and still weaken their residency file without meaning to.

Where the systems collide

The complexity emerges not from the systems themselves, but from how they intersect in a single person's life.

For example:

- Immigration may allow you six months
- The IRS may treat you as a tax resident after three years of consistent patterns
- Your province may restrict health coverage if your presence drops below the required threshold

Each system is correct within its own definition. The conflict appears only when a Snowbird assumes that one rule governs everything.

Why this matters

Snowbirds who rely on a single guideline — usually the six-month myth — leave themselves exposed. A stable cross-border lifestyle requires understanding how the systems overlap and where they diverge.

Key Idea

You are navigating multiple systems, not one.
Clarity comes from seeing how each interprets your choices.

Case Study: When a Routine Snowbird Pattern Becomes a Risk

When people run into trouble with cross-border rules, it rarely happens all at once. More often, the issues build quietly over a period of years. The following case reflects a pattern I have seen repeatedly — small decisions accumulating meaning until they create consequences no one expected.

Case Study: Alan and Margaret's Winter Routine

Alan and Margaret, a retired couple from Edmonton, had been spending winters in Arizona for nearly a decade. Their routine felt stable. They stayed about four and a half months each year, always returned to Canada in the spring, and never believed they were anywhere close to a problem. They had heard the familiar guidance from neighbors: stay under six months and you're fine.

For years, nothing challenged that assumption.

When Margaret needed surgery in late autumn one year, their winter plans shifted slightly. They arrived later than usual and extended their spring return by a few weeks so she could complete her recovery in a warmer climate. The extra days felt harmless. They had never gone over six months, and they didn't now.

What they didn't realize was that the IRS was not looking at this season alone.

Their pattern over the previous two years — roughly 140 to 150 days each winter — placed them close to the substantial presence threshold. The added weeks from Margaret's recovery pushed their three-year total past 183 days.

They had no intention of becoming U.S. tax residents. Yet by the IRS test, that is where they now stood.

Where confusion turned into risk

The issue came to light when their travel insurance provider asked for exact dates of entry and exit to verify eligibility. Neither Alan nor Margaret had kept detailed records. They had always estimated. Their approximations no longer aligned with the requirements of the insurer, the IRS, or their accountant.

When they attempted to reconstruct their travel dates, everything depended on memory, flight confirmations, and stamped passports that did not cover every crossing.

How the tools changed the outcome

If Alan and Margaret had been using the Snowbirds U.S. Day Tracker App, their dates and cumulative IRS totals would have been visible months earlier. The app would have shown how close they were to the threshold and flagged the risk as it developed. They could have filed the necessary Form 8840 proactively, preserving their Canadian tax residency and avoiding unnecessary exposure.

Instead, they filed late, at their accountant's urging, after a stressful reconstruction process.

Why this case matters

Their situation was not the result of carelessness. It was the outcome of a long-standing misconception and a lack of tools to make the rules clear. Their story reflects the reality for many Snowbirds: the lifestyle is enjoyable, but the systems behind it require attention.

Key Idea

Small changes in a travel pattern can shift your status dramatically when viewed through the IRS formula. Tools exist to detect that shift early — long before it becomes a problem.

Looking Ahead: The Next Chapter

Chapter Two explains how Snowbirds unintentionally become U.S. tax residents under the IRS Substantial Presence Test. It breaks down the three-year weighted formula, illustrates how common travel patterns can cross the 183-day threshold, and outlines the filing consequences if no exception is claimed. The chapter then explains Form 8840 (Closer Connection Exception), including eligibility requirements, annual filing expectations, and key limitations. It also emphasizes accurate day tracking, provides practical avoidance steps, and uses short case studies to show tax, provincial health coverage, and immigration-related risks tied to day-count mistakes.

CHAPTER TWO
HOW SNOWBIRDS ACCIDENTALLY BECOME U.S. TAX RESIDENTS— AND HOW TO AVOID IT

In This Chapter, You Will Learn...

- How the **IRS Substantial Presence Test (SPT)** works and why the six-month rule is a myth.
- The **12-month rolling calendar** and why it matters for U.S. immigration and tax purposes.
- Why accurate **day tracking** is essential for staying compliant with U.S. and Canadian laws.
- How **Form 8840 (Closer Connection Exception)** helps Snowbirds maintain Canadian residency.
- Practical steps for **avoiding U.S. tax residency** — from day tracking to understanding the nuances of the IRS formula.
- The **role of the Snowbirds U.S. Day Tracker™ App** in helping Snowbirds stay on top of their U.S. day-counts and avoid surprises at the border.

THE IRS SUBSTANTIAL PRESENCE TEST (SPT)

When Snowbirds think about their time in the United States, they often operate under the assumption that a simple rule governs their stay: spend fewer than 182 days in the U.S., and you're fine. This belief, passed down through informal channels, is widespread but fundamentally **wrong**.

The Truth About the IRS Substantial Presence Test

The IRS doesn't use a six-month rule. Instead, it relies on a **weighted formula** that calculates the total number of days you've spent in the U.S. over the past three years. It doesn't matter whether you've been there for 120 days, 150 days, or 180 days each year. The IRS **looks at a rolling total**, with days from previous years contributing at a **reduced value**.

Here's how the formula works:

- All the days you spend in the U.S. this year count as **full days**.
- One-third of the days from last year count.
- One-sixth of the days from the year before count.

The IRS adds these up. If the total equals or exceeds **183 days**, then **you're considered a U.S. tax resident**, even if you've never stayed longer than 182 days in any given year.

Why It's More Dangerous Than You Think

Many Snowbirds spend **120 to 150 days** in the U.S. each year. They believe this keeps them well under the IRS threshold. However, under the **three-year weighted formula**, that's **not the case**. Here's the hidden danger:

If you've been spending 130 days in the U.S. each year, you may believe you're safe. But add up the numbers:

- 130 days this year
- 43 days from last year
- 21 days from the year before

This adds up to **194 days**, which **triggers U.S. tax residency**, despite never having stayed more than 182 days in any given year.

The Snowbird Trap: You Don't See It Coming

Most Snowbirds don't even realize they've triggered the IRS Substantial Presence Test until it's too late.

- They don't track the exact number of days they've spent in the U.S.
- They rely on approximations or calendars that don't account for the exact IRS formula.
- They often assume that being under six months every year is enough.

But the IRS doesn't care about six months. It looks at the pattern of travel over multiple years.

Key Fact: The SPT Isn't Just About the Number of Days You Spend in the U.S.

What's crucial here is that even if you've spent 120–150 days in the U.S. consistently, you are still at risk if your total day count over the three-year period **exceeds 183**.

What Happens If You Trigger U.S. Tax Residency

If you exceed the IRS threshold and do not file for an exception, the consequences are significant:

- You must file a U.S. tax return (Form 1040), even if all your income is Canadian.
- You report worldwide income, which can result in double taxation.
- You will need to complete complex IRS forms to report your global financial activity.
- You will become subject to U.S. tax laws — whether you want it or not.

Key Idea

The IRS Substantial Presence Test doesn't rely on the six-month rule.

It's based on the cumulative pattern of days you spend in the U.S. over multiple years.

What to do next?

Managing Your Days and Filing Form 8840

If you have exceeded the IRS threshold, **Form 8840 (Closer Connection Exception)** can help you maintain your Canadian residency for tax purposes. This form proves that, despite meeting the day count, you have stronger ties to Canada. It's simple to file, but many Snowbirds miss it because they don't track their days properly.

How the Snowbirds U.S. Day Tracker™ App Helps

By entering your entry and exit dates manually, the Snowbirds U.S. Day Tracker™ App calculates your cumulative totals and shows you where you stand. No guessing. No approximations. You can see when you are approaching the IRS threshold and take action early. The app is built this way on purpose: many Snowbirds limit mobile data while in the U.S., and we chose not to build GPS tracking into the app.

How Form 8840 Protects Canadians — and When It Doesn't

One of the most effective tools available to Snowbirds who risk triggering U.S. tax residency under the **Substantial Presence Test (SPT)** is **Form 8840**, known as the **Closer Connection Exception**. This simple form allows you to claim that despite meeting the day-count threshold, your closer ties remain with Canada, not the U.S.

What Form 8840 Does

Form 8840 is a protection mechanism that prevents Snowbirds from being automatically classified as U.S. tax residents. By filing this form, you:

- **Confirm your closer connection to Canada**: You must demonstrate that your primary home, family, and personal connections are based in Canada.
- **Avoid double taxation**: If the IRS considers you a U.S. tax resident, you could be required to file U.S. taxes and report worldwide income, which could lead to double taxation.

The form is straightforward, but it **must be filed every year** you are at risk of exceeding the SPT threshold. It's not a one-time exemption — it's an annual requirement for Snowbirds who spend more than a short period in the U.S. but want to maintain Canadian tax residency.

When Form 8840 Doesn't Help

While **Form 8840** can prevent you from being considered a U.S. tax resident, it's not a magic bullet for every situation. The form only works if you meet certain conditions:

- **You must have a stronger connection to Canada than the U.S.** This means more than just owning a home in Canada. Your family, job, and financial ties must all be based in Canada. If you've started working remotely for a U.S. employer or left behind strong ties in Canada, this form will not protect you.
- **Your days in the U.S. must not exceed 183 days,** unless you qualify for additional exceptions (such as the closer connection exception itself). If you're spending more than six months in the U.S., you're likely already beyond the scope of what Form 8840 can protect.

If you fail to meet these conditions, Form 8840 will not shield you from U.S. tax residency, and you'll be required to file as a U.S. tax resident.

Why Form 8840 Is Crucial for Snowbirds

Filing Form 8840 is essential because:

- It establishes **your tax residency** for the year in question.

- It ensures **you won't be taxed as a U.S. resident** if you're genuinely connected to Canada, saving you from additional tax burdens.
- It **protects your health coverage** under provincial plans in Canada, preventing unnecessary complications when you file your taxes.

In short, it's a critical tool that Snowbirds should use proactively, not reactively.

Key Idea

Form 8840 is your lifeline to maintaining Canadian tax residency despite spending time in the U.S. It's simple to file, but you must do it every year if you are at risk of meeting the SPT.

The Challenge: Remembering to File It

Filing Form 8840 is often an afterthought for Snowbirds who don't track their days closely. Too often, they discover the need for the form only after they've exceeded the 183-day threshold — and by then, it's too late.

How the Snowbirds U.S. Day Tracker™ App Solves This Problem

To avoid this trap, the Snowbirds U.S. Day Tracker™ App lets you record your travel dates manually, then calculates your totals so you have the information you need to file Form 8840 ahead of time. It does not rely on GPS tracking, and it does not require constant data usage to be useful.

With the app, you'll know exactly where you stand with the IRS. No more guesswork. No more relying on memory. The app gives you a detailed breakdown of your days in the U.S., ensuring you don't exceed the threshold and that you have the necessary data to file Form 8840 before it's too late.

Key Idea

Day tracking is essential to avoid the IRS residency trap. The Snowbirds U.S. Day Tracker™ App makes it straightforward by calculating everything from the dates you enter, so you can stay organized and avoid missing your filing deadlines.

Why Accurate, Real-Time Day Tracking Is the Only Reliable Defense

For Snowbirds, the most reliable defense against falling into U.S. tax residency is accurate, real-time tracking of days spent in the United States. Yet, many Canadians still rely on **mental estimates**, **flight records**, or **approximate calendar calculations** to track their U.S. days. These methods often leave too much room for error, which can lead to unexpected consequences — sometimes years down the line.

The Risk of Imbalance: Too Much Reliance on Memory

Relying on memory or rough estimates can be problematic for several reasons:

- **People forget specific dates**: While it may seem easy to recall the rough time frame of a trip, day-count accuracy is essential. Often, people mistakenly include days they were in the U.S. but didn't track, or they forget to account for travel days or short stays.

- **Flight records don't cover everything**: Flight tickets show arrival and departure, but they don't capture the true duration of a stay. For instance, a Snowbird may have entered the U.S. on January 5th, but returned home for a few days mid-January. These gaps aren't always clear from flight records alone.

- **Calendar approximations are unreliable**: Many Snowbirds use a physical or online calendar to mark the days they are in the U.S. The problem here is that small mistakes in day-counting can add up over time. A missed weekend or unaccounted-for extended stay can push the total day count past 183 without realizing it.

Why the IRS Cares

The IRS does not accept approximations. Under the Substantial Presence Test, the **exact number of days** spent in the U.S. is the **only** factor that matters. A Snowbird who estimates their days and ends up exceeding the limit by a few days can be caught by surprise when the IRS considers them a U.S. tax resident.

A minor oversight in tracking days doesn't just affect taxes. It can trigger a domino effect, causing issues with immigration, provincial health coverage, and other cross-border matters. If day-counts are off by a significant margin, it could lead to **unnecessary complications** — from filing U.S. tax returns to losing Canadian residency benefits.

The Critical Need for Real-Time Tracking

In this system, **real-time day tracking** is non-negotiable. Snowbirds cannot afford to estimate, guess, or rely on memory. With accurate, up-to-date tracking, you know exactly how many days you've spent in the U.S., and can take the appropriate steps **before the threshold is crossed.**

How the Snowbirds U.S. Day Tracker™ App Solves This Problem

This is exactly why the Snowbirds U.S. Day Tracker™ App was created. It calculates your rolling totals from the travel dates you enter, so you can stop relying on handwritten notes, flight records, or rough guesses. Because many Snowbirds limit U.S. data usage, the app is designed to be effective without GPS tracking or constant data access.

The app automatically adjusts your day-count, showing exactly where you stand at any given time, so you never have to wonder if you're on track. It also provides **alerts** when you approach the 183-day threshold, giving you ample time to adjust travel plans, file Form 8840, or take other necessary steps before triggering U.S. tax residency.

Key Idea

Accurate, real-time day tracking is the foundation of managing your cross-border life effectively. The Snowbirds U.S. Day Tracker™ App makes it easy to stay compliant with U.S. and Canadian tax laws.

How the App Works

The app works by:

- **You manually enter** your entry and exit dates (quickly, in one place).
- The app **calculates your cumulative days** over a rolling 3-year period using the IRS formula.
- It **flags when your totals are approaching key thresholds**, such as the 183-day limit.
- It provides a clear day count, so you can make informed decisions about your travel.
- **It does not use GPS tracking, and it is designed to be practical even for Snowbirds who limit mobile data in the U.S.**

Key Idea

Proactive day tracking removes guesswork, and makes it easier to stay compliant with both U.S. and Canadian tax rules.

Real Snowbird Case Studies That Show How Quickly Mistakes Happen

Real-life examples are the most effective way to understand how the IRS Substantial Presence Test (SPT) and day-counting mistakes can cause problems. Snowbirds don't need to "intend" to become U.S. tax residents — they just need to spend enough time in the U.S. over multiple years, and the IRS will apply its formula, regardless of intent. In this section, we will look at some **real scenarios** that show how quickly a pattern can trigger unexpected consequences, and how the **Snowbirds U.S. Day Tracker™ App** can prevent those mistakes.

CASE STUDY 1: JOHN AND SUSAN'S UNEXPECTED TAX BILL

John and Susan, a retired couple from Vancouver, had been spending their winters in Florida for the last decade. Every year, they estimated their days in the U.S. They used their flight tickets and marked dates on a calendar, assuming that as long as they stayed under 182 days in any given year, they would be fine.

What went wrong:

After a few years, John and Susan noticed they were spending slightly more time in Florida each year, typically staying around 140 to 150 days annually. However, they never considered the cumulative effect of those days.

When it was time to file their Canadian tax returns, their accountant asked about their U.S. presence. That's when they discovered the **IRS Substantial Presence Test** applied, and their **cumulative days** from the previous years added up to **over 183** — triggering U.S. tax residency. They were required to file a **U.S. tax return** and report their global income.

How the app helped:

Had they been using the Snowbirds U.S. Day Tracker™ App, they would have been notified of the potential risk long before filing season arrived. The app would have given them an accurate day count based on the dates they entered, and it would have shown them early that their totals were creeping toward the IRS threshold. With this early warning, they could have filed **Form 8840** to maintain their Canadian tax residency.

Key takeaway:

Accurate tracking of days is the only way to ensure you don't trigger the SPT unintentionally. The app would have kept John and Susan from facing an unexpected tax bill.

CASE STUDY 2: SARAH'S HEALTH COVERAGE LOSS

Sarah, a snowbird from Calgary, had been wintering in Arizona for nearly five years. She owned a condo in Scottsdale and spent about 130 days per year in the U.S. However, her primary focus was always on enjoying her retirement. She kept a Canadian driver's license, used her provincial health card, and filed her taxes in Canada.

What went wrong:

When Sarah spent a particularly long winter in Arizona, staying 145 days, her provincial health plan in Canada reached out for confirmation of her residency status. Sarah didn't realize that by spending more than **7 months (approximately 210 days) in the U.S. over two years**, she was **no longer eligible for provincial health coverage**. She was shocked to learn that her extended stays had put her in danger of losing Canadian health benefits.

How the app helped:

Had Sarah used the Snowbirds U.S. Day Tracker™ App, she would have seen exactly where her days stood over the last three years. The app would have provided clear alerts when her travel patterns were at risk of affecting her residency status — both for tax and health purposes. By using the app to track her days, she could have adjusted her plans earlier to maintain her health coverage in Canada.

Key takeaway:

Day tracking not only helps avoid U.S. tax issues but also protects your **health benefits** and Canadian residency status. Accurate records and alerts allow for proactive planning.

CASE STUDY 3: MARK'S REMOTE WORK DILEMMA

Mark, a successful business consultant from Toronto, had been spending winters in the U.S. since his retirement. However, Mark continued working remotely for a Canadian company, conducting online meetings and sending reports while in Florida.

What went wrong:

Even though Mark was only working a few hours a week, he had unknowingly violated the **conditions of his visitor visa**. He had been working from the U.S. for several years under the **B-2 Visitor Visa**, which strictly prohibits engaging in any form of employment while in the country. He assumed because he wasn't working for a U.S. company, he was exempt.

When CBP questioned him during his last entry, they flagged his activities. He was advised to stop working remotely while in the U.S. and warned that continuing this pattern could jeopardize his ability to re-enter the country.

How the app helped:

Mark's case could have been avoided with the Snowbirds U.S. Day Tracker™ App. By using the app to track his days, Mark would have been alerted to potential issues with his **visa status**.

The app's real-time tracking could have helped him adjust his behavior — ending his remote work while in the U.S. or shortening his stay to ensure he remained in compliance with visa rules.

Key takeaway:

Tracking **not only** protects your tax status but also ensures **compliance with immigration laws**. The app helps Snowbirds stay informed and avoid unintentional violations.

Key Idea

Day tracking is essential for Snowbirds not just to manage taxes but also to maintain their status, health coverage, and immigration compliance. The Snowbirds U.S. Day Tracker™ App provides clarity in real-time, ensuring you stay ahead of potential issues.

How to Avoid Accidentally Becoming a U.S. Tax Resident

The IRS Substantial Presence Test (SPT) can catch even the most diligent Snowbird off guard. One of the most frustrating aspects of this test is that it doesn't rely on your intent. You can spend what you consider a reasonable amount of time in the U.S. — a few months each year — and still become a U.S. tax resident without realizing it.

The good news is that **you can take steps to avoid this trap**, and it starts with **managing your days** and filing the correct forms on time.

Step 1: Be Disciplined with Day Tracking

First and foremost, **track your days accurately**. Without knowing exactly how many days you've spent in the U.S., it's nearly impossible to avoid crossing the 183-day threshold over multiple years.

You should keep a record of every **single trip** you make to the U.S.

This means no relying on vague approximations, flight records alone, or rough estimates. **Precise tracking** is the foundation of everything.

How the Snowbirds U.S. Day Tracker™ App Helps

The **Snowbirds U.S. Day Tracker™ App** was created specifically for this purpose. By entering your travel dates into the app, it automatically calculates your days spent in the U.S. over the past three years, based on the IRS's weighted formula. It also gives you **real-time updates** so you can see how close you are to the threshold before it becomes an issue.

The app helps you:

- Keep track of **exact days spent** in the U.S.
- See your total day count over a **rolling three-year period**.
- Receive **alerts** when your day count is approaching the 183-day limit.

This allows you to **make adjustments** well before you cross the threshold.

Step 2: File Form 8840

If you're at risk of exceeding the Substantial Presence Test threshold, filing **Form 8840 (Closer Connection Exception)** can be your lifeline. This form allows you to maintain your Canadian tax residency, even if you exceed the IRS threshold.

When to File Form 8840

- **File every year**: You must file Form 8840 each year you are at risk of triggering U.S. tax residency, even if you don't exceed the threshold.
- **Prove your Canadian ties**: The form requires you to provide proof of your **closer connection to Canada**. This includes having a home in Canada, family living there, and other primary ties.
- **Avoid double taxation**: Filing this form ensures that you don't get taxed twice — once by the U.S. and once by Canada — on the same income.

It's important to remember that **Form 8840 must be filed annually**. This is not a one-time exemption but a proactive filing that protects your Canadian residency.

Step 3: Manage Your Travel Patterns

Even with careful day tracking and Form 8840, your travel pattern plays a significant role in whether or not you will face issues with the IRS.

The Importance of Limiting Your Days

While staying under 183 days is the primary guideline, maintaining **flexibility** in your travel schedule can help you avoid crossing the threshold.

Here are a few key practices to consider:

- **Target a day count of 121–130**: This range keeps you safe without risking the substantial presence threshold. It also offers a bit of flexibility for unplanned travel.

- **Be mindful of longer stays**: Staying longer than necessary could push your total days over the 183 thresholds in future years. If you're planning an extended stay, be aware of the cumulative effect over multiple years.
- **Avoid back-to-back long stays**: If you visit the U.S. year after year without taking breaks or reducing the duration of your trips, the cumulative effect will increase your risk of crossing the IRS threshold.

Step 4: Consult a Professional if Necessary

If your travel patterns are complex, or you're unsure how your day counts will affect your U.S. tax residency status, it's important to **consult with a cross-border tax specialist**. They can help ensure you're tracking your days correctly and filing the necessary forms to avoid U.S. tax residency.

Key Idea

Proactive management of your travel days, consistent tracking, and filing Form 8840 annually are the best ways to avoid accidentally becoming a U.S. tax resident.

The Snowbird's New Reality: How to Stay in Control of Your U.S. Day Count

The IRS Substantial Presence Test (SPT) is a complicated system, but once you understand how it works and how to manage it, staying compliant becomes far less daunting. The key to avoiding U.S. tax residency is simple: **accurate day tracking, filing Form 8840 on time, and being mindful of your travel patterns.**

But here's the truth: many Snowbirds do not realize how easily they can get caught in the SPT trap until it's too late. The real question is: **How can you ensure you stay ahead of the system instead of being caught off guard?**

What We've Learned So Far

1. **The SPT doesn't use the six-month rule.**
   The IRS counts your days across a rolling three-year period using a weighted formula. A simple six-month assumption is not enough. You must account for the cumulative effect of your days in the U.S.

2. **Day tracking is critical.**
   Whether you track it manually or through an app, **knowing the exact number of days** you spend in the U.S. each year is your first line of defense. Without precise tracking, you risk unknowingly exceeding the 183-day threshold.

3. **Form 8840 protects you — if you file it correctly and on time.**
   The form allows you to claim that your ties to Canada are stronger than your ties to the U.S. However, it only works if you **file it every year** you are at risk of exceeding the threshold, and **you meet the conditions** for a closer connection to Canada.

4. **Your travel patterns matter.**
   If you consistently spend long periods in the U.S. each year, your total day count will eventually reach the critical threshold. Keeping your stays within the safe range (121–130 days per year) provides more flexibility, but **consistency is key.**

5. **The Snowbirds U.S. Day Tracker™ App is your best ally.**
   By using the app, you can ensure you're never caught off guard. The app **uses the travel dates you enter to calculate your cumulative totals** and **shows you when you are approaching key thresholds**, so you can adjust plans and handle forms before problems start.

The Key Takeaway

Tracking your days accurately is the most effective way to protect your U.S. and Canadian tax residency status. The Snowbirds U.S. Day Tracker™ App simplifies this process and provides you with the tools you need to stay compliant, avoid surprises, and keep your travel plans on track.

What Snowbirds Should Do Now

- **Start tracking your days immediately**, even if you haven't had issues before.
- If you are already approaching the SPT threshold, **file Form 8840** as soon as possible.
- Be **mindful of your travel patterns** and aim for 121–130 days per year, if possible, to give yourself some flexibility.
- **Use the Snowbirds U.S. Day Tracker™ App** to stay on top of your day count and ensure you're never surprised by a potential tax residency issue.

Looking Ahead: The Next Chapter:

Chapter Three explains how U.S. immigration evaluates Snowbirds using a 12-month rolling calendar rather than a calendar year. It shows why border decisions are driven by travel patterns and perceived intent, not just the length of a single trip. The chapter identifies common red-flag patterns, explains how discretion operates (including shortened stays and notes on file), and clarifies why frequent short trips can be as risky as one long stay. It closes with practical planning principles and the role of consistent manual day tracking in preserving visitor status.

CHAPTER THREE
THE 12-MONTH ROLLING CALENDAR

The Immigration Rule Snowbirds Ignore — But Cannot Afford To

In This Chapter, You Will Learn...

- How U.S. immigration evaluates Snowbirds using a **12-month rolling calendar**, not a calendar year.
- Why immigration focuses on **travel patterns**, not just the length of individual trips.
- The types of travel behavior that commonly raise **questions or concerns at the border**.
- How **immigration discretion** works and why similar travelers can receive different outcomes.
- Why frequent short trips can be just as risky as one long stay.
- How consistent, manual **day tracking** gives Snowbirds visibility and control before issues arise.
- Practical ways to plan U.S. travel that preserves your status as a **visitor**, not a resident.

The Rule That Changes Everything

By the time most Snowbirds begin to feel confident about their cross-border planning, they believe the hardest part is behind them. They have learned that the six-month rule is unreliable.

They understand the IRS Substantial Presence Test. They may even be tracking their days more carefully than they ever have before.

That sense of relief is understandable. It is also premature.

What many Snowbirds do not realize is that **immigration operates on a completely different clock**, one that has nothing to do with calendar years, tax filings, or weighted formulas. Immigration looks backward, not forward. It evaluates what you have already done, not what you plan to do. And it does so using a rolling window that quietly reshapes how your travel history appears at the border.

This is where the 12-month rolling calendar enters the picture.

Unlike tax rules, which focus on residency status, immigration rules are concerned with **intent**. Officers are not asking whether you owe taxes. They are asking a more basic question: Are you visiting, or are you effectively living in the United States without permission?

To answer that, immigration does not rely on a January-to-December count. It looks at **the last 365 days from the moment you arrive at the border**. Every U.S. day within that period matters. Long stays matter. Short stays matter. Multiple trips matter. Patterns matter most of all.

This is why Snowbirds are often confused when they are questioned, limited, or denied entry even though they believe they have followed the rules. From their perspective, nothing has changed. From immigration's perspective, everything has.

The challenge is that this rule is rarely explained clearly. It is not posted on government websites in a way that feels practical. It is not discussed in casual Snowbird conversations. And it is almost never mentioned until the moment it becomes a problem.

This chapter exists to make that rule visible.

Before we go any further, one distinction matters. **The 12-month rolling calendar is not a tax rule.** It does not replace the IRS Substantial Presence Test, and it does not interact with it directly. It operates alongside it. A Snowbird can be fully compliant for tax purposes and still raise serious immigration concerns based solely on how much time they have spent in the United States over the past year.

Understanding this difference changes how you plan. It shifts your focus from isolated trips to overall patterns. And it explains why so many Snowbirds feel blindsided at the border even when they believe they have done everything right.

In the sections that follow, we will break this rule down carefully. You will see how immigration interprets travel history, what patterns raise concern, and why tracking only one system creates unnecessary risk. You will also see how proper day tracking, done deliberately and consistently, gives you visibility long before an officer ever raises a question.

This is the rule most Snowbirds never hear about.

It is also the rule that protects your ability to enter the United States at all.

Why Immigration Cares About Patterns, Not Promises

Snowbirds often believe that clear intentions should be enough. They are visiting. They have return tickets. They have homes in Canada. They are not trying to work or stay permanently. From their point of view, the story seems simple.

Immigration does not evaluate the story the same way.

At the border, officers are trained to look past stated plans and focus instead on **observable behavior**. They are not measuring what you say you intend to do. They are assessing what your travel history suggests you are already doing.

This is why patterns matter more than promises.

A single long stay rarely causes concern on its own. What draws attention is repetition. Returning year after year for similar lengths of time. Staying for extended stretches, leaving briefly, and coming back again. Spending more time in the United States than in Canada over a rolling period. These behaviors, taken together, begin to resemble residence rather than visitation.

Immigration officers do not need proof that you are trying to live in the United States. They only need to see enough evidence that your pattern no longer fits the definition of a visitor.

This distinction is critical. Many Snowbirds assume that as long as each individual trip appears reasonable, the overall picture will be fine. In reality, immigration looks at the **entire sequence**, not the individual pieces.

The 12-month rolling calendar makes this assessment sharper. An officer can review your last year of entries and exits and see exactly how much time you have spent inside the United States, regardless of how those days were spread across multiple trips. From that perspective, frequent shorter stays can look just as concerning as one long stay.

What complicates matters further is that Snowbirds often plan their travel around tax rules or health coverage requirements, not immigration thresholds. They may shorten a stay to avoid tax residency while unintentionally increasing the frequency of trips. They may return to Canada briefly to reset a calendar year, not realizing that immigration's clock never resets.

This is where misunderstandings begin to stack up. Snowbirds believe they are being cautious. Immigration sees a pattern that suggests dependence on U.S. time.

It is also important to understand that officers have discretion. Two people with identical day counts may receive different outcomes depending on how their overall pattern appears, how clearly, they can explain their travel, and how consistent their story is with their history. This is not a system that rewards assumptions. It rewards preparation.

Knowing this changes how Snowbirds should think about planning. It is no longer enough to ask, "How long can I stay this trip?" The more important question becomes, "What does my last 12 months look like as a whole?"

In the next section, we will examine the specific patterns that tend to raise concern at the border, and why they often surprise people who believed they were staying well within the rules.

The Travel Patterns That Raise Red Flags

Most Snowbirds who run into trouble at the border are genuinely surprised. They did not stay the full six months. They did not work. They did not overstay a visa. From their point of view, nothing they did felt excessive.

From immigration's point of view, the pattern told a different story.

Certain travel behaviors consistently draw attention, not because they violate a single rule, but because they suggest a shift away from temporary visitation. These patterns do not announce themselves as problems. They develop quietly over time, often reinforced by habits that feel practical or even responsible.

One of the most common red flags is **long, repeated seasonal stays**. Spending four or five months in the United States every winter may feel reasonable, especially if it aligns with weather, housing arrangements, or health considerations. When that same pattern repeats year after year, immigration begins to question whether the stay is still temporary in nature.

Another concern is **minimal time spent back in Canada between U.S. visits**. Some Snowbirds leave the United States for a short period, only to return again soon after. While each entry may be lawful on its own, the overall picture can suggest that Canada has become a place of brief interruptions rather than a primary home.

Frequency matters as much as duration. **Multiple short trips**, spread throughout the year, can accumulate into a level of presence that raises questions. Immigration does not view ten short trips differently from one long stay if the total time adds up to the same result.

Lifestyle indicators also play a role. Officers may consider whether you maintain a vehicle in the United States, keep personal belongings at a U.S. residence, or hold ongoing commitments that require you to be physically present. These factors do not independently determine outcomes, but they contribute to how your travel history is interpreted.

Even language can influence perception. Telling an officer that you plan to "spend the whole winter" or that you "live here part of the year" may feel casual, but those words carry weight.

Immigration evaluates not only what you do, but how you describe your relationship with the country.

What makes these patterns particularly difficult is that none of them feels like a clear violation. Snowbirds often believe they will receive a warning before consequences appear. In reality, the first sign of concern may be additional questioning, a shortened stay, or a notation added to your travel record.

At that point, the pattern already exists.

This is why accurate awareness matters. Snowbirds who understand how immigration reads their travel history can adjust behavior before it becomes an issue. Those who rely on assumptions often discover the problem only after discretion has already been exercised.

In the next section, we will look at how immigration discretion works in practice, and why two Snowbirds with similar travel histories can have very different experiences at the border.

How Discretion Works at the Border

For Snowbirds, one of the most unsettling aspects of U.S. immigration is that there is no single outcome that applies to everyone. Two travelers can arrive on the same day, with similar travel histories, and leave with very different results. This inconsistency often feels unfair, but it is built into the system by design.

Immigration officers are given broad discretion. Their role is not limited to checking stamps or counting days. They are tasked with making a judgment call based on the totality of a person's circumstances at the moment of entry.

That assessment happens quickly, often in a matter of minutes.

Officers may review your recent travel history, ask about the purpose of your visit, and listen carefully to how you describe your time in the United States. They are trained to notice hesitation, contradictions, or explanations that do not align with the record in front of them. None of this requires wrongdoing. It requires only uncertainty.

What surprises many Snowbirds is that discretion does not mean unpredictability. Patterns guide decisions. If your history suggests repeated long stays, limited time in Canada, or a routine that resembles residence, an officer may shorten your authorized stay even if they allow you to enter. In some cases, they may ask for proof of ties to Canada or documentation that supports your stated plans.

This is often the moment when Snowbirds realize that immigration decisions are not negotiated in real time. You cannot explain your way out of a pattern that has already formed. You can only live with how that pattern is interpreted.

Another important point is that discretion accumulates. Notes entered into border systems remain there. A shortened stay or additional questioning becomes part of your record. Future entries may be evaluated through the lens of those prior interactions, even if your behavior has not changed.

Many Snowbirds assume that if they are polite and cooperative, discretion will work in their favor. Courtesy matters, but preparation matters more. Officers respond best to travelers who understand the rules that apply to them and can explain their plans clearly, consistently, and confidently.

This is where visibility becomes an advantage. Knowing how many days you have spent in the United States over the last 12 months, and being able to explain how your travel fits within a broader plan, changes the dynamic. It shifts the interaction from uncertainty to clarity.

In the next section, we will explore how Snowbirds can regain control of that clarity, and why tracking your days deliberately is not about limiting freedom, but preserving it.

Regaining Control Through Visibility

Most immigration problems do not begin with a dramatic moment at the border. They begin much earlier, in the quiet space where assumptions replace information. Snowbirds plan trips based on habit, comfort, or convenience, rarely stopping to examine how those choices accumulate over time.

The turning point comes when visibility replaces guesswork.

Visibility does not mean memorizing rules or anticipating every possible question an officer might ask. It means knowing, with certainty, what your recent travel history looks like and how it fits within the immigration framework. When Snowbirds understand their own patterns, they can adjust them before discretion ever comes into play.

This is where day tracking becomes practical rather than theoretical. Immigration does not respond to intentions. It responds to records. Knowing exactly how many days you have spent in the United States over the past twelve months allows you to plan your next trip with purpose instead of hope.

For many Snowbirds, this requires a shift in mindset. Tracking days is often seen as restrictive, something that limits spontaneity. In reality, the opposite is true. When you can see your numbers clearly, you gain flexibility. You know when you can stay longer and when it is wiser to shorten a visit. You recognize patterns early rather than explaining them later.

Manual tracking, done consistently, is enough. What matters is accuracy and follow-through. Recording entry and exit dates, reviewing totals periodically, and understanding how those totals appear under a rolling calendar gives you control over your travel narrative.

Tools exist to make this process easier, not more intrusive. By entering dates and reviewing cumulative totals, Snowbirds can maintain awareness without relying on memory, receipts, or approximations. The goal is not automation for its own sake. The goal is confidence.

When Snowbirds arrive at the border knowing where they stand, their answers are clearer. Their plans are easier to explain. Their travel history aligns with their stated purpose. That alignment is what reduces friction.

In the final section of this chapter, we will bring these ideas together and show how thoughtful planning, consistent tracking, and an understanding of immigration patterns work as a single system rather than isolated rules.

Staying a Visitor in Practice, Not Just in Theory

At its core, U.S. immigration is not asking Snowbirds to prove perfection. It is asking them to remain visitors in a way that is visible, consistent, and credible. The difficulty is that many Snowbirds rely on informal rules that were never designed to guide long-term, repeated travel.

The 12-month rolling calendar changes how immigration views time. It replaces the comfort of annual resets with a continuous evaluation of presence. Once Snowbirds understand this, the rules stop feeling arbitrary. They begin to look like a system that rewards awareness and penalizes assumptions.

Staying a visitor means more than keeping individual trips short. It means maintaining balance. Time in the United States should not quietly outweigh time at home. Travel should not resemble a routine that repeats without pause. Your pattern should make sense when viewed as a whole, not just one entry at a time.

This is why coordination matters. Tax rules, immigration rules, and health coverage requirements do not operate together, but your life does. Decisions made to satisfy one system can unintentionally strain another. Without visibility, Snowbirds are left reacting instead of planning.

Accurate day tracking plays a central role in avoiding that reaction. By recording travel dates and reviewing cumulative totals, Snowbirds can see risks forming long before they reach the border. This awareness allows adjustments to happen early, when options still exist.

The goal is not to reduce time spent enjoying the United States. The goal is to protect the ability to return. Snowbirds who understand how immigration interprets their travel history are better positioned to preserve flexibility, reduce stress, and avoid difficult conversations at the border.

As this chapter closes, one idea should remain clear. Immigration does not operate on casual guidelines. It operates on patterns. When Snowbirds plan with those patterns in mind, the lifestyle they value becomes far easier to sustain.

Looking Ahead: The Next Chapter

Chapter Four explains what Canadians should consider when buying, holding, and selling U.S. property as Snowbirds. It focuses on ownership structure and how that choice affects taxes, estate exposure, probate, and long-term flexibility. The chapter outlines post-purchase obligations, the differences between personal use, rental use, and mixed use, and why documentation and reporting discipline matter across both countries. It also explains FIRPTA withholding at sale and why exit strategy planning should start at the time of purchase, not when you list the property.

CHAPTER FOUR
BUYING, HOLDING, AND SELLING U.S. PROPERTY AS A CANADIAN SNOWBIRD

In this chapter, you will learn:

- Why buying U.S. real estate as a Snowbird is a **cross-border planning decision**, not just a lifestyle upgrade.
- How **ownership structure** affects taxes, estate exposure, and long-term flexibility.
- What obligations are triggered **after you buy**, even if the property is never rented.
- How **personal use, rental use, and mixed use** create different reporting and compliance requirements.
- Why U.S. property ownership can influence **immigration perception**, even though it provides no immigration rights.
- How **FIRPTA withholding** works when selling U.S. property and why it often surprises Canadian sellers.
- Why planning for your **exit strategy** should begin at purchase, not at sale.

For many Snowbirds, buying property in the United States feels like a natural next step. After learning how to manage travel days, taxes, and immigration limits, ownership can seem like stability. A place to return to. A sense of belonging. A long-term plan.

What often goes unnoticed is that **real estate changes your cross-border profile immediately**, even before you move in or earn a dollar from the property.

This is where Snowbirds tend to underestimate the stakes.

Canadians are allowed to buy U.S. real estate. There are no citizenship restrictions. No residency requirements. No special visas needed. On the surface, the transaction looks familiar: an offer, a deposit, a closing date. That apparent simplicity is precisely what causes trouble later.

Buying is easy.

Owning is where complexity begins.

The moment you hold U.S. property, you introduce new layers of exposure that affect **tax reporting, estate planning, immigration perception, and long-term financial coordination**. These issues do not arise because something is done incorrectly. They arise because many Snowbirds never realize how many systems are triggered by ownership alone.

The First Decision That Matters: Ownership Structure

Before price, before location, before ocean views, the most important decision is **how the property will be owned**.

Many Canadians default to purchasing in their personal name or jointly with a spouse. In many cases, this is appropriate. Problems arise when Snowbirds are encouraged to use structures they do not fully understand, such as U.S. LLCs, partnerships, or layered ownership arrangements that promise flexibility but introduce unintended consequences.

Ownership structure affects:

- Exposure to U.S. estate tax
- Canadian reporting obligations
- Probate requirements in the United States
- FIRPTA withholding when the property is sold
- Ongoing compliance costs

This is not an area where complexity equals sophistication. In fact, unnecessary structure is one of the fastest ways to create tax and legal friction across borders.

Key Point:

The wrong ownership structure can cost tens of thousands of dollars over time, even if the property itself performs well.

Financing Reality for Canadian Buyers

Financing U.S. property as a Canadian is possible, but it rarely mirrors the experience at home.

Down payments are typically higher, often ranging from **20 to 35 percent**. Interest rates may be less favorable. Documentation requirements are stricter. Currency exchange adds another variable that can quietly amplify costs or gains depending on timing.

These realities do not make U.S. property unattractive. They simply mean that the numbers must be reviewed carefully, not emotionally. A purchase that looks affordable at closing can feel very different once exchange rates, carrying costs, and long-term obligations are fully understood.

Why Location Is More Than a Lifestyle Choice

Snowbirds often compare U.S. locations based on weather, community, or amenities. From a planning perspective, **state-level differences matter just as much**.

Property taxes, insurance requirements, condo association rules, rental restrictions, and closing procedures vary significantly from one state to another. What works smoothly in Arizona may look entirely different in Florida or Hawaii.

This is why real estate decisions cannot be separated from jurisdictional knowledge. Listings do not explain how local rules affect foreign owners. Agents are rarely positioned to address cross-border consequences. That responsibility ultimately rests with the buyer.

A Shift in Perspective

At this stage, Snowbirds often realize that real estate ownership is not just about acquiring a property. It is about entering a new phase of cross-border planning.

Owning U.S. property does not grant immigration rights. It does not extend permitted stay. It does not simplify tax rules. In some cases, it increases scrutiny rather than reducing it.

This does not mean Snowbirds should avoid buying. It means they should buy with awareness.

In the next section, we will examine what happens **after the purchase**, and why holding U.S. property introduces long-term considerations that deserve regular review rather than one-time decisions.

What Ownership Triggers After the Purchase

For many Snowbirds, the closing date feels like the finish line. Papers are signed. Keys are handed over. The stress of the transaction fades, replaced by the comfort of having a place of their own in the United States.

From a cross-border perspective, that moment is not an ending. It is a starting point.

U.S. property ownership activates obligations that exist quietly in the background, regardless of whether the home is rented, occupied, or sitting empty. These obligations are not always immediate, which is why they are often missed. But they accumulate, and when they surface later, they tend to do so all at once.

Property Ownership and U.S. Tax Filing

The first assumption Snowbirds often make is that if no income is earned, no U.S. tax filing is required. That is sometimes true, but not always, and it should never be assumed.

Owning property alone does not automatically require a U.S. tax return. However, the moment the property produces income, even briefly, reporting obligations are triggered. Short-term rentals, seasonal leases, or cost-sharing arrangements can all create taxable events under U.S. law.

Just as important is how that income is classified. The IRS treats rental income differently depending on elections made at the outset, expenses claimed, and the degree of involvement in managing the property. These decisions affect not only U.S. taxes, but also Canadian reporting and foreign tax credits.

Key Point:

The way rental income is reported in the first year often sets the tone for every year that follows.

The FIRPTA Issue Most Snowbirds Discover Too Late

Many Canadians are unaware of **FIRPTA**, the Foreign Investment in Real Property Tax Act, until they are preparing to sell.

Under FIRPTA, the U.S. government requires withholding at the time of sale when a foreign person disposes of U.S. real estate. This withholding is not a tax bill. It is a prepayment against potential tax owed. Still, the amount can be significant, often **15 percent of the gross sale price**, not the gain.

This surprises Snowbirds who expected taxes to apply only to profits. FIRPTA does not work that way.

Advance planning can reduce or eliminate unnecessary withholding, but only if addressed before the sale closes. Once the transaction is complete, options narrow quickly.

Estate Exposure Begins Immediately

One of the least discussed consequences of U.S. property ownership is **estate tax exposure**.

Unlike Canada, the United States applies estate tax based on asset location, not residency alone. U.S.-situated property owned by a Canadian can be subject to U.S. estate tax upon death, even if the individual never became a U.S. resident.

This does not mean every Snowbird will face estate tax. Treaty protections exist. Exemptions may apply. But eligibility depends on asset values, ownership structure, and coordination with Canadian estate planning.

What matters is timing. Estate planning done after purchase is often reactive. Estate planning considered before or immediately after purchase is far more effective.

Insurance and Liability Considerations

Holding U.S. property introduces liability exposure that differs from Canadian norms. Insurance requirements, coverage limits, and exclusions vary by state and by property type. Condominium policies, homeowners' associations, and flood zones add layers that are easy to overlook.

Liability does not require rental activity. Accidents can happen even when the property is occupied only by the owner or guests. Understanding coverage boundaries is essential, especially when assets span multiple jurisdictions.

How Ownership Affects Immigration Perception

While owning property does not grant any immigration privileges, it can influence how travel patterns are perceived.

Immigration officers may consider property ownership as one factor among many when evaluating intent. A home, combined with extended stays and repeated visits, can strengthen the appearance of residence rather than visitation.

This does not mean ownership is a problem. It means ownership increases the importance of **balanced travel patterns** and clear explanations at the border.

A Broader Responsibility

Once Snowbirds own U.S. property, their cross-border life becomes more interconnected. Tax filings, estate planning, insurance, immigration, and currency management begin to overlap. Decisions made in one area influence outcomes in another.

This is why property ownership should never be treated as an isolated decision. It is a long-term commitment that benefits from periodic review rather than one-time planning.

In the next section, we will look at **rental use and personal use**, and why how you use your U.S. property matters just as much as the fact that you own it.

Personal Use, Rental Use, and the Lines Snowbirds Often Cross Without Realizing

Once Snowbirds own U.S. property, the question is no longer just *whether* they own it, but **how they use it**. That distinction matters more than many people expect.

From a distance, personal use and rental use appear straightforward. You stay when you want. You rent when you are not there. The reality is more layered, especially when usage patterns interact with tax rules, reporting obligations, and immigration perception.

Personal Use Is Not Neutral

Using your U.S. property exclusively for personal stays does not eliminate complexity. In fact, it can quietly increase exposure if not planned carefully.

Extended personal use often leads to:

- Longer continuous stays
- Fewer breaks between visits
- Travel patterns that resemble seasonal residence

Individually, none of these are prohibited. Collectively, they can shift how your presence is interpreted. Ownership combined with long personal use makes it harder to maintain the clear profile of a visitor, particularly when reviewed under a rolling 12-month window.

This is where visibility matters again. Snowbirds who own property tend to underestimate how ownership subtly changes their travel behavior over time.

Rental Use Creates Immediate Tax Obligations

The moment a U.S. property is rented — even for a short period — reporting requirements are triggered.

Rental income must be reported in the United States. Expenses must be allocated properly. Elections made in early years affect depreciation, future capital gains, and FIRPTA outcomes when the property is sold.

Just as importantly, rental income must also be reported in Canada, with foreign tax credits applied correctly. Errors here are rarely intentional. They usually stem from misunderstanding how the two systems interact.

Key Fact:

Rental use changes the tax character of the property, even if income is modest or infrequent.

Mixed Use Requires Discipline

Many Snowbirds fall into mixed use without realizing it. They rent occasionally. They stay occasionally. They allow friends or family to use the property. Each of these choices affects classification, expense deductibility, and reporting requirements.

Mixed use is not a problem by default. Poor documentation is.

This is where Snowbirds often struggle. They remember roughly when they were present. They approximate rental periods. Over time, those approximations weaken their records and create inconsistencies between tax filings and actual use.

Where the App Fits — and Where It Doesn't

The Snowbirds U.S. Day Tracker™ App does not manage rental income, property tax, or estate exposure. It was never designed to.

What it *does* help with is **clarity around presence.**

For Snowbirds who own property, manual day tracking becomes more important, not less. Ownership increases scrutiny. Longer stays become more tempting. Patterns shift gradually.

By recording entry and exit dates consistently, Snowbirds can:

- See how ownership affects travel behavior over time
- Maintain balance between personal use and overall presence
- Avoid unintentionally creating patterns that resemble residence

The app supports awareness. It does not replace planning.

Immigration Perception Tightens With Ownership

Immigration officers do not treat property ownership as a violation. But they do consider it context.

A Snowbird who owns property, stays for extended periods, and returns frequently will be evaluated differently than someone without those ties. Clear records, balanced travel, and confident explanations matter more once ownership enters the picture.

This is why Snowbirds who buy property must be more deliberate, not more casual.

A Shift From Lifestyle to Responsibility

At this stage, Snowbirds often realize that ownership is not just an upgrade in comfort. It is a shift in responsibility.

Personal use decisions affect tax exposure. Rental decisions affect reporting. Travel decisions affect immigration perception. None of these operate independently.

In the next section, we will examine **exit strategies**, including selling U.S. property, FIRPTA withholding, and why planning for the end of ownership is just as important as planning for the beginning.

Selling U.S. Property: The Rules That Apply When You Exit

Most Snowbirds spend far more time planning how to buy U.S. property than how to sell it. The purchase feels optional. The exit feels distant. For many, it is years away.

From a planning perspective, that delay is costly.

Selling U.S. real estate as a Canadian is not simply the reverse of buying it. Different rules apply. Different authorities become involved. And decisions made years earlier can shape outcomes in ways that are difficult to unwind at the end.

FIRPTA: The Rule That Governs the Sale

When a Canadian sells U.S. real estate, the transaction falls under the **Foreign Investment in Real Property Tax Act (FIRPTA)**. This law requires the buyer to withhold a portion of the sale proceeds and remit it to the U.S. government.

The key point that surprises most Snowbirds is this: **The withholding is based on the gross sale price, not the gain.**

Typically, the withholding rate is **15 percent of the total sale price**, regardless of whether the property was profitable, marginal, or even sold at a loss. FIRPTA treats the withholding as a prepayment against potential tax owed, not a final assessment.

This distinction matters. A Snowbird selling a property for $800,000 could see $120,000 withheld at closing, even if the actual tax liability is far lower.

Why Withholding Is Not the Same as Tax

FIRPTA withholding does not mean you owe that full amount in tax. It means the U.S. government is holding funds until the final tax return is filed and the actual liability is calculated.

In many cases, Snowbirds are entitled to a refund. The problem is timing. Refunds can take months, sometimes longer, and the withheld funds are unavailable during that period.

Advance planning can reduce or eliminate unnecessary withholding, but only if addressed before the sale closes. Once funds are withheld and transferred, flexibility disappears.

The Role of Planning Before the Sale

Many Snowbirds learn about FIRPTA after accepting an offer. At that stage, options narrow quickly. Proper planning may involve applying for a withholding certificate, coordinating timing, or ensuring records support a reduced withholding amount.

These steps are not complicated, but they are time-sensitive. Waiting until after the sale is rarely effective.

Capital Gains and Cross-Border Reporting

In addition to FIRPTA, capital gains must be reported in both the United States and Canada. While tax treaties and foreign tax credits help prevent double taxation, coordination matters.

The way the property was used, depreciated, and reported over the years affects the final calculation. Errors made earlier often surface at sale, when correcting them becomes more difficult and more expensive.

Estate Considerations at the Point of Sale

For some Snowbirds, the decision to sell is driven by estate planning rather than lifestyle. Changes in family structure, health, or asset values may prompt a reassessment.

Selling during lifetime versus holding until death can produce very different outcomes. Estate exposure, probate requirements, and tax treatment vary depending on timing and ownership structure.

These are not decisions to rush. They are decisions to evaluate deliberately.

Why Exit Planning Belongs at the Beginning

The most important takeaway from this section is simple: **Exit planning should begin when ownership begins.**

Snowbirds who understand FIRPTA, capital gains exposure, and estate implications early can make ownership decisions that preserve flexibility later. Those who postpone these conversations often discover constraints when they are least welcome.

In the next section, we will step back and look at how all of these elements — ownership, use, taxation, immigration, and exit — fit together into a single cross-border framework that Snowbirds can manage with confidence rather than reaction.

Seeing U.S. Property as Part of a Larger Cross-Border Picture

By the time Snowbirds reach this point, one truth should be clear: U.S. real estate does not exist in isolation. It sits inside a web of tax rules, immigration considerations, estate exposure, insurance requirements, and long-term planning decisions that stretch across borders.

Problems arise when property ownership is treated as a lifestyle upgrade rather than a structural commitment.

Each choice made along the way carries forward. How the property is owned influences estate outcomes. How it is used affects tax filings. How long it is occupied shapes immigration perception. How it is sold determines cash flow at exit. None of these decisions stand alone, even when they are made years apart.

What catches Snowbirds off guard is not complexity itself, but timing. Consequences rarely appear immediately. They surface later, often at moments when flexibility is limited. A sale. A health event. A border issue. A change in family circumstances. By then, earlier assumptions are difficult to undo.

This is why U.S. property ownership benefits from periodic review rather than one-time planning. Circumstances evolve. Asset values change. Travel patterns shift. What made sense at purchase may need adjustment five or ten years later.

Ownership does not require perfection. It requires awareness.

Snowbirds who treat property as one element of a coordinated cross-border plan tend to experience fewer surprises. They ask better questions earlier. They document decisions more carefully. They recognize when professional advice is warranted rather than reactive.

The goal is not to discourage ownership. It is to align it with the rest of your cross-border life so that enjoyment does not come at the cost of unnecessary risk.

Looking Ahead: The Next Chapter

Chapter Five explains what Snowbirds need to understand about healthcare in the United States before a medical event occurs. It outlines why U.S. medical costs can be financially disruptive, why provincial health coverage provides only limited out-of-country reimbursement, and why travel medical insurance is essential for extended stays. The chapter highlights common policy failure points, including pre-existing condition definitions, stability periods, coverage duration, renewal rules, and gaps in coverage. It also explains how insurance choices interact with travel patterns and immigration scrutiny, and provides practical steps for selecting coverage that matches real Snowbird travel behavior.

CHAPTER FIVE
HEALTHCARE IN THE U.S.: WHAT SNOWBIRDS MUST UNDERSTAND BEFORE THEY NEED IT

In This Chapter, You Will Learn...

In this chapter, you will learn how healthcare planning fits into the broader reality of Snowbird life and why misunderstandings in this area create some of the most expensive cross-border mistakes.

Specifically, this chapter will show you:

- Why Canadian provincial health coverage offers little protection in the United States
- How U.S. medical costs quickly overwhelm out-of-country coverage limits
- What travel medical insurance actually covers, and where it commonly falls short
- Why pre-existing condition clauses and stability requirements matter more than coverage limits
- How insurance duration, renewal rules, and coverage gaps affect extended stays
- How healthcare decisions interact with travel patterns and immigration scrutiny

- Practical ways to choose coverage that reflects how Snowbirds truly live, not ideal assumptions
- How proactive healthcare planning reduces financial risk without creating unnecessary anxiety

This chapter is designed to help you approach healthcare planning with clarity and discipline, so medical protection supports your Snowbird lifestyle rather than becoming a source of stress or uncertainty.

The Reality of U.S. Healthcare Costs

For Snowbirds, no risk is more commonly underestimated than medical costs in the United States. Taxes feel abstract. Immigration feels procedural. Healthcare, for many, feels unlikely. Something that happens to other people.

That assumption is dangerous.

The United States does not operate on a public healthcare model. Every test, every treatment, every night in a hospital is billed individually. There is no provincial safety net. There is no negotiated national rate. There is only the invoice.

What makes this especially difficult for Snowbirds is that **the most expensive events are rarely predictable**. People do not plan heart attacks, strokes, falls, infections, or accidents. They happen in ordinary moments, often during what feels like a routine winter stay.

Understanding the cost environment is not about fear. It is about realism.

Why U.S. Healthcare Is Structurally Expensive

U.S. healthcare costs are high because the system is built around private delivery and private billing. Hospitals, physicians, specialists, imaging centers, and emergency services all bill separately. Pricing varies widely by location, provider, and urgency of care.

There is no universal cap on charges. There is no automatic coverage for non-residents. Payment is expected regardless of nationality.

To put this into context, common costs in the United States include:

- Emergency room visits that routinely run into several thousand dollars
- Diagnostic imaging that can cost more than an entire Canadian vacation
- Hospital stays that accumulate charges daily, not weekly
- Intensive care that can exceed tens of thousands of dollars per day
- Medical evacuation flights that rival the cost of a small home renovation

These numbers are not exceptional cases. They are typical.

Key Fact:

A single serious medical event in the U.S. can exceed the value of a lifetime of travel savings.

Why Canadian Expectations Don't Translate

Snowbirds often underestimate U.S. costs because they subconsciously apply Canadian assumptions. In Canada, emergency care does not involve price negotiation. Treatment is delivered first. Billing, if it exists at all, is secondary.

In the United States, hospitals are required to treat emergencies, but they are also entitled to payment. Proof of insurance is requested early. Credit card authorization is common. Deposits are not unusual.

This difference matters because Snowbirds arrive healthy, active, and confident. They do not feel like medical risk profiles. The system does not care how healthy you felt yesterday.

The Financial Exposure Is Total

Without insurance, medical bills are not limited to disposable income. They can reach:

- Registered retirement savings
- Tax-free savings
- Home equity
- Lines of credit
- Family support

The damage is not always immediate, but it is lasting. Snowbirds who absorb large medical bills often scale back travel permanently, not by choice, but by necessity.

This is why healthcare risk belongs at the centre of cross-border planning, not at the margins.

Why This Chapter Matters

Everything that follows in this chapter is designed to answer a single question:

How do Snowbirds protect themselves from a system that assumes private responsibility for every dollar of care?

To do that, we need to understand what Canadian provincial plans actually cover, where they stop, and why travel medical insurance is not optional for extended stays in the United States.

That is where we turn next.

What Your Canadian Provincial Health Plan Really Covers

One of the most persistent misunderstandings among Snowbirds is the belief that Canadian provincial health coverage offers meaningful protection outside the country. The card is valid. Contributions are paid. Coverage exists at home. It feels reasonable to assume that some level of protection travels with you.

In practice, it barely does.

Canadian provincial health plans were never designed to cover care in foreign healthcare systems, particularly one as costly as that of the United States. Any out-of-country coverage that exists is limited, outdated, and quickly overwhelmed by real-world medical billing.

The Limits of Provincial Coverage

While each province administers its own plan, the structure is largely the same across Canada. Out-of-country coverage is typically restricted to **fixed daily maximums** that reflect historical Canadian billing rates, not current U.S. costs.

Those limits often include:

- A capped daily amount for hospital care
- Minimal coverage for emergency physician services

- No meaningful coverage for diagnostic imaging, follow-up care, or extended treatment

In many cases, provincial plans reimburse **only a few hundred dollars per day**, regardless of the actual cost of treatment. That reimbursement is paid to the patient, not the provider, and usually only after documentation is submitted and reviewed.

Key Fact:

Provincial health coverage typically pays a fraction of U.S. medical costs, leaving Snowbirds responsible for the overwhelming majority of expenses.

Why This Gap Is So Dangerous

Snowbirds rarely encounter this gap until it matters. A hospital does not negotiate based on what your province might reimburse. Charges accrue immediately and aggressively. The difference between what is billed and what is reimbursed becomes the patient's responsibility.

A short emergency room visit can exceed the annual out-of-country coverage limit. A hospital stay of even one or two days can surpass it many times over.

This disconnect creates a false sense of security. Snowbirds believe they are partially protected when, in reality, the exposure is almost total.

Provincial Residency Requirements Add Another Layer

Maintaining provincial health coverage requires more than holding a valid card. Provinces impose **minimum physical**

presence requirements to remain eligible. Exceeding allowable time outside Canada can result in loss or suspension of coverage.

These requirements vary by province, but they generally limit the amount of time residents can be absent in a given year. Snowbirds who spend extended periods in the United States must be mindful of these thresholds.

Losing provincial coverage does not only affect care at home. It also complicates private insurance eligibility and reinstatement. Coverage gaps can emerge quietly and only become visible when a claim is denied.

What Provincial Coverage Does Not Do

It is equally important to understand what provincial plans do not cover when you are outside Canada:

- No direct billing arrangements with U.S. hospitals
- No negotiation of charges
- No evacuation or repatriation coverage
- No coordination of care
- No protection against catastrophic billing

In short, provincial health plans do not function as travel insurance.

Why This Matters Before You Buy Insurance

Many Snowbirds approach travel medical insurance as a supplement to provincial coverage. That framing is backwards. Private travel insurance is the primary protection. Provincial coverage, if anything, plays a secondary and often symbolic role.

Understanding this distinction is critical. It shapes how Snowbirds evaluate insurance limits, deductibles, exclusions, and duration of coverage.

In the next section, we will examine **travel medical insurance itself**: what it covers, what it excludes, and why not all policies are created equal for extended stays in the United States.

Travel Medical Insurance: What Snowbirds Need and Why

By the time Snowbirds begin shopping for travel medical insurance, most already sense that it is important. What they often lack is a clear understanding of **what kind of insurance they actually need**, and why some policies fail precisely when they are needed most.

Travel medical insurance is not a formality. It is a financial firewall. And like any firewall, its effectiveness depends on how it is built.

Why Basic Coverage Is Not Enough

Many Snowbirds purchase insurance the way they purchase flights or accommodations. They compare prices. They skim limits. They assume that higher numbers mean better protection.

In reality, coverage quality is defined less by headline figures and more by **conditions and exclusions**.

Policies designed for short vacations are often ill-suited for extended Snowbird stays. They may cap coverage periods, restrict renewals, or impose limitations that only become visible after a claim is filed.

Key Fact:

Insurance that looks sufficient on paper can be inadequate in practice if it does not match the length and nature of your stay.

The Pre-Existing Condition Problem

One of the most common reasons claims are denied involves pre-existing conditions. Snowbirds are often surprised by how broadly this term is defined.

A condition does not need to be severe or recent to be considered pre-existing. Medication adjustments, diagnostic tests, or physician visits within a look-back period can all affect eligibility. Even conditions that feel stable can fall outside coverage if disclosure requirements are not met precisely.

This is not a matter of interpretation after the fact. It is a matter of contract language agreed to before departure.

Understanding how pre-existing conditions are defined, how stability periods work, and how disclosure obligations are enforced is essential. Assumptions here are expensive.

Coverage Duration and Continuity

Another overlooked issue is duration. Snowbirds often purchase insurance for an initial stay, planning to extend or renew later if needed. Not all policies allow this. Some treat extensions as new policies, resetting underwriting requirements.

Gaps in coverage, even brief ones, can invalidate claims tied to events that occur shortly after reinstatement. This creates exposure that Snowbirds rarely anticipate.

For extended stays, continuity matters as much as limits.

Emergency Does Not Mean Everything Is Covered

Insurance typically covers emergencies, not convenience. The distinction matters.

An emergency is defined by immediacy and necessity. Follow-up care, elective procedures, or treatment deemed non-urgent may fall outside coverage even if they arise from an emergency event.

Authorization requirements also play a role. Many policies require notification within specific time frames. Failure to comply can limit reimbursement, regardless of medical outcome.

Medical Evacuation and Repatriation

One area where policy differences are especially stark is evacuation coverage.

Medical evacuation is not a luxury. It is a logistical necessity when care must be coordinated across borders. Costs can be substantial, particularly if specialized transport or long-distance flights are required.

Not all policies offer the same evacuation terms. Coverage limits, approved destinations, and decision authority vary widely. Understanding who decides when evacuation occurs, and where you are taken, is critical.

Choosing Coverage That Matches Reality

The best travel medical insurance for Snowbirds is not the cheapest. It is the most appropriate.

That means:

- Coverage limits that reflect real U.S. costs

- Policies designed for extended stays, not short trips
- Clear definitions of pre-existing conditions
- Continuous coverage without forced gaps
- Robust evacuation provisions

This is not an area for shortcuts. The risk is not inconvenience. The risk is financial damage that follows you home.

In the next section, we will look at **how insurance, immigration rules, and travel patterns intersect**, and why coverage decisions must be coordinated with how long and how often Snowbirds spend time in the United States.

How Healthcare, Travel Patterns, and Immigration Intersect

Snowbirds often treat healthcare planning as a standalone task. Insurance is purchased. Documents are printed. The box feels checked. What is rarely considered is how **healthcare coverage interacts with travel behavior and immigration rules**, especially over extended or repeated stays.

These systems do not coordinate with one another. But the consequences of decisions made in one area often surface in another.

Longer Stays Increase Medical Exposure

Time matters. The longer a Snowbird remains in the United States, the greater the likelihood that medical care will be needed. This is not about declining health. It is about probability.

Extended stays increase exposure to:

- Accidents and falls

- Seasonal illnesses
- Chronic condition flare-ups
- Environmental factors such as heat or air quality

Insurance policies are built around time. Coverage periods, renewal rules, and eligibility requirements all assume a defined duration. Snowbirds who stay longer than planned often discover that extending coverage is not automatic and may come with restrictions.

Insurance Decisions Influence Travel Decisions

Insurance coverage can quietly shape travel behavior. Some Snowbirds shorten stays because coverage runs out. Others stay longer than intended because returning home for coverage resets feels disruptive.

Neither approach is ideal if it is reactive.

Travel patterns influenced by insurance limitations can unintentionally create immigration concerns. Multiple short trips to maintain coverage or repeated extensions that lengthen overall presence can alter how travel history appears under a rolling 12-month review.

Medical Events Can Affect Border Decisions

A significant medical event can change how future entries are evaluated. Immigration officers may ask about recent hospitalizations, ability to support oneself, or plans for ongoing care.

While medical issues do not automatically affect admissibility, they can become relevant if they suggest extended stays, dependency on U.S. systems, or uncertainty about departure plans.

Snowbirds who have experienced serious medical care in the U.S. are often surprised to find that future entries involve more detailed questioning.

Evacuation and Timing Matter

Medical evacuation decisions are not made in isolation. They involve physicians, insurers, and logistics providers. Timing matters, especially when evacuation crosses borders.

Delays, authorization issues, or disputes about medical necessity can prolong stays unexpectedly. These extensions may affect both insurance coverage and immigration posture.

Planning for these scenarios does not mean expecting the worst. It means recognizing that medical events can reshape timelines quickly.

Why Coordination Is Essential

Healthcare planning cannot be separated from travel planning. Insurance terms influence how long you can safely stay. Travel duration influences medical exposure. Medical events influence future border interactions.

Snowbirds who understand this intersection plan differently. They align insurance coverage with realistic travel patterns. They build buffer time into stays. They avoid reactive extensions that create confusion across systems.

This coordination reduces stress at moments when clarity matters most.

In the next section, we will look at **practical steps Snowbirds can take to protect themselves**, including how to evaluate policies, plan coverage windows, and avoid common mistakes that lead to denied claims or coverage gaps.

Protecting Yourself Without Overreacting

By the time Snowbirds reach this point, the risks associated with U.S. healthcare should feel clear, but not overwhelming. The goal of understanding these systems is not to create fear. It is to replace casual assumptions with informed choices.

Healthcare planning works best when it is deliberate, not reactive.

Most problems arise when insurance decisions are made late, renewed automatically without review, or stretched beyond their intended use. Snowbirds who encounter difficulties rarely ignored insurance entirely. More often, they misunderstood the limits of the coverage they had.

Start With Realistic Travel Planning

Effective healthcare protection begins with honesty about how you travel. Length of stay matters. Frequency matters. Patterns matter.

Insurance should be purchased to match how you actually live, not how you hope to travel in a best-case scenario. Short-term policies layered together rarely perform as well as coverage designed for extended stays.

Planning coverage around realistic timelines reduces the likelihood of rushed extensions, coverage gaps, or denied claims.

Read Policies for Conditions, Not Comfort

Marketing language is designed to reassure. Policy language determines outcomes.

Snowbirds should focus less on promotional summaries and more on:

- Definitions of pre-existing conditions
- Stability periods and look-back windows
- Coverage duration limits
- Renewal and extension rules
- Evacuation authority and destinations

Understanding these elements before departure is far easier than disputing them after a claim.

Avoid the "I'll Deal With It Later" Trap

Many Snowbirds assume they will revisit insurance if circumstances change. Unfortunately, medical events often occur without warning. Once care is required, options narrow quickly.

Proactive planning creates space to make choices calmly. Reactive planning forces decisions under pressure.

Coordinate Coverage With the Rest of Your Cross-Border Plan

Insurance does not exist in isolation. It interacts with:

- Immigration rules and length of stay
- Provincial health coverage eligibility
- Travel flexibility
- Financial planning and asset protection

When insurance decisions align with travel patterns and residency requirements, Snowbirds experience fewer disruptions and less uncertainty.

The Quiet Advantage of Preparation

Well-prepared Snowbirds rarely talk about insurance because it works quietly in the background. They travel confidently. They stay within coverage limits. They return home without financial surprises.

This chapter is not about eliminating risk. It is about **containing it**.

Looking Ahead: The Next Chapter

Chapter Six explains cross-border estate planning for Snowbirds who own U.S. property or other U.S.-situs assets. It outlines how U.S. estate tax rules can apply to Canadians, what assets trigger exposure and filing requirements, and how these rules interact with Canada's deemed disposition at death. The chapter also explains why treaties may reduce double taxation but do not eliminate compliance burdens, and why liquidity planning is often the difference between orderly administration and forced asset sales. It closes with common planning mistakes and practical structures that help families manage cross-border estates more predictably.

CHAPTER SIX
ESTATE PLANNING ACROSS THE BORDER: PROTECTING YOUR FAMILY AND YOUR ASSETS

In This Chapter, You Will Learn...

In this chapter, you will learn why estate planning is one of the most overlooked yet consequential aspects of Snowbird life, and how cross-border ownership changes what happens after death in ways many families do not expect.

Specifically, this chapter will show you:

- Why owning U.S. assets exposes Canadians to **U.S. estate tax**, regardless of residency
- What qualifies as **U.S.-situs property** and why modest holdings can trigger filing requirements
- How Canada's **deemed disposition rules** apply at death and interact with U.S. estate tax
- Why tax treaties reduce double taxation but do not remove complexity or filing obligations
- How liquidity shortages can force asset sales at the worst possible time
- The most common estate planning mistakes Snowbirds make, even with professional advice

- Practical planning structures that reduce estate risk and simplify administration
- Why cross-border estate planning must be reviewed as Snowbird life evolves

This chapter is designed to help Snowbirds move from uncertainty to preparation, so families are protected from unnecessary cost, delay, and stress when it matters most.

The Overlooked Risk of Snowbird Life

Most Canadians who build a Snowbird lifestyle think carefully about travel, taxes, and healthcare. Estate planning, however, often remains an afterthought. Not because people are careless, but because death feels distant, abstract, and unrelated to winter travel plans.

That assumption creates one of the most serious vulnerabilities in cross-border living.

If you own U.S. property, hold U.S. investments, or spend meaningful time in the United States, your estate does not remain purely Canadian. Whether you intend it or not, your affairs are exposed to two legal systems, two tax regimes, and two probate processes that operate independently of one another.

This reality surprises families when it matters most.

Why Cross-Border Estates Are Different

A Canadian estate is usually settled within a familiar framework. Assets are valued. Taxes are calculated. Probate follows a known process. The rules are complex, but they are at least unified.

The moment U.S. assets enter the picture, that unity disappears.

The United States assesses estate tax based on where assets are located, not where the owner lived. Canada, on the other hand, treats death as a deemed sale of worldwide assets and applies capital gains tax accordingly. These systems do not coordinate their outcomes. They apply their rules independently and expect compliance on both sides.

What feels like a single estate becomes two overlapping estates with different definitions, timelines, and obligations.

The Scale of the Exposure Is Commonly Misunderstood

Many Canadians assume U.S. estate tax only applies to the ultra-wealthy. That belief is rooted in headlines about large exemptions available to U.S. citizens. Those exemptions do not apply to Canadians.

For non-U.S. citizens, the exemption on U.S.-situs assets is extremely limited. A modest condominium, a U.S. investment account, or even shares of U.S. companies held through a Canadian brokerage can be enough to trigger filing requirements and tax exposure.

This is not a loophole. It is how the system is designed.

What Makes This Risk So Difficult to See

Estate problems do not surface gradually. They appear suddenly, often after death, when families are least equipped to deal with complexity.

Assets can become frozen.
Probate can stretch across jurisdictions.
Taxes can be assessed before heirs have access to funds.

Decisions may be made under pressure, with limited information and no opportunity to restructure ownership.

The planning window closes the moment an estate event occurs.

Why This Chapter Matters

This chapter exists because cross-border estate issues are preventable, but only if they are addressed deliberately and early. The goal is not to eliminate every tax or complication. The goal is to avoid unnecessary exposure, delays, and forced decisions that erode wealth and strain families.

In the sections that follow, we will examine:

- How U.S. estate tax applies to Canadians
- How Canadian deemed disposition creates double-tax risk
- What actually happens when a Canadian dies with U.S. assets
- The most common planning mistakes Snowbirds make
- Practical structures that reduce risk and improve outcomes

This is not theoretical planning. It is preparation for real outcomes that occur every year.

When Snowbirds understand how estate rules work across borders, they gain the ability to protect their families from confusion, cost, and conflict. That clarity begins here.

Understanding U.S. Estate Tax for Canadians

For many Snowbirds, U.S. estate tax is the least understood aspect of cross-border planning. It is often dismissed as something that applies only to Americans or to extremely wealthy families. Both assumptions are wrong.

U.S. estate tax applies based on **where assets are located**, not where the owner lives or pays income tax. For Canadians who own U.S.-situs assets, this distinction is critical.

What Counts as a U.S.-Situs Asset

From the U.S. perspective, certain assets are considered to have a U.S. location regardless of the owner's nationality. These include:

- Real estate located in the United States
- Shares of U.S. corporations, even if held through a Canadian brokerage
- U.S.-based investment accounts
- Certain U.S. partnership interests

It does not matter whether the asset produces income or whether it was purchased for personal use. Location determines exposure.

Why the Exemption Is So Misleading

News coverage often highlights large U.S. estate tax exemptions, sometimes exceeding ten million dollars. Those exemptions apply to U.S. citizens and domiciliaries.

Canadians are treated differently.

For non-U.S. citizens, the base exemption on U.S.-situs assets is minimal. While treaty provisions between Canada and the United States can provide some relief, they do not eliminate the issue. They introduce calculations, proportional exemptions, and filing requirements that must be navigated carefully.

Key Fact:

Many Canadians with relatively modest U.S. assets are required to file a U.S. estate tax return, even if no tax is ultimately owed.

When Tax Is Actually Payable

Whether tax is payable depends on several factors:

- The value of U.S.-situs assets
- The value of worldwide assets
- How treaty exemptions apply proportionally
- How assets are owned and titled

Because the calculation considers worldwide net worth, a Snowbird with significant Canadian assets can face U.S. estate tax exposure even if U.S. assets represent only a portion of the estate.

This is where planning often breaks down. People focus on the U.S. property itself and overlook how the broader estate influences the calculation.

The Filing Obligation Matters Even Without Tax

One of the most underestimated aspects of U.S. estate tax is the filing requirement. A U.S. estate tax return may be required even when no tax is payable.

Failure to file can result in:

- Penalties
- Delays in releasing U.S. assets
- Increased scrutiny of estate valuations
- Additional administrative cost

Filing is not optional when thresholds are met. It is part of the price of owning U.S. assets as a non-resident.

Why This Often Catches Families Off Guard

Estate tax exposure is rarely discussed during the purchase of U.S. property. The transaction feels straightforward. Title is registered. Taxes are paid. Ownership feels complete.

The consequences, however, sit quietly in the background.

They emerge later, when families are grieving, timelines are compressed, and options are limited. At that point, even well-intentioned heirs may struggle to untangle obligations they did not know existed.

This is why understanding U.S. estate tax is not about pessimism. It is about responsibility.

In the next section, we will look at **how Canadian tax rules interact with U.S. estate tax**, and why death can trigger obligations on both sides of the border at the same time.

When Two Tax Systems Apply at the Same Time

For Canadians with U.S. assets, the most difficult part of estate planning is not understanding each country's rules individually. It is understanding what happens when **both systems apply at once**.

Canada and the United States do not settle estates together. They apply their own laws independently, based on different principles, and on different timelines. When death occurs, both systems activate simultaneously.

Canada's Deemed Disposition Rule

Canada does not levy an estate tax in the traditional sense. Instead, it treats death as if the individual sold all of their assets at fair market value immediately before death.

This "deemed disposition" triggers capital gains tax on:

- Real estate
- Investment portfolios
- Business interests
- Certain foreign assets

The tax is payable by the estate, often before assets are distributed to heirs.

For Snowbirds with U.S. property or investments, this means Canadian capital gains tax is triggered regardless of whether the asset is actually sold.

The U.S. Estate Tax Operates Differently

While Canada taxes gains, the United States taxes **asset value**. U.S. estate tax applies to the fair market value of U.S.-situs assets at death, not to the gain realized.

These two approaches do not cancel each other out. They stack.

A single U.S. property can generate:

- Canadian capital gains tax under deemed disposition
- U.S. estate tax exposure based on asset value
- Filing obligations in both countries

Why Treaties Help but Do Not Eliminate the Risk

The Canada–U.S. tax treaty exists to reduce double taxation, not to eliminate complexity. It can provide credits or proportional exemptions, but it does not erase filing requirements or administrative burdens.

Treaty relief requires:

- Accurate valuations
- Proper filings on both sides of the border
- Timely elections and disclosures

Mistakes or delays can reduce available relief.

Liquidity Becomes a Critical Issue

Taxes triggered at death often become payable before assets are sold. This creates a liquidity problem.

If an estate consists largely of real estate or long-term investments, heirs may be forced to:

- Sell assets quickly
- Borrow against property
- Advance personal funds
- Accept unfavorable terms under pressure

These outcomes are rarely planned. They arise because liquidity was not considered alongside tax exposure.

Why Families Struggle at This Stage

Heirs are often encountering cross-border rules for the first time. They are managing grief, paperwork, deadlines, and unfamiliar systems simultaneously.

Without advance planning, families may not know:

- Which professionals to contact
- Which filings take priority

- How long assets will be inaccessible
- What options exist to reduce exposure

This is why cross-border estate planning cannot wait until later. Later is often too late.

In the next section, we will examine **common planning mistakes Snowbirds make**, and why even well-intentioned decisions can increase risk rather than reduce it.

The Most Common Estate Planning Mistakes Snowbirds Make

Cross-border estate problems rarely come from neglect. They come from **partial planning**. People address one issue while unknowingly creating another.

Snowbirds tend to be thoughtful planners. They travel deliberately. They manage finances carefully. Yet estate exposure still appears because decisions are made in isolation, without seeing how the systems overlap.

Mistake One: Assuming a Canadian Will Is Enough

A Canadian will governs Canadian assets well. It does not automatically address U.S. property or U.S.-situs investments in a way that simplifies administration south of the border.

Without proper coordination, heirs may face:

- Separate probate proceedings
- Conflicting executor authority
- Delays in accessing U.S. assets

A Canadian will is necessary, but it is not always sufficient on its own.

Mistake Two: Buying U.S. Property Without Planning the Exit

Many Snowbirds plan carefully for purchase and ownership. Few plan for sale or transfer at death.

Exit planning is not pessimistic. It is practical.

Without it, families may face:

- Forced sales under time pressure
- FIRPTA withholding
- Unexpected tax filings
- Limited flexibility in how assets are distributed

The best time to plan the exit is at acquisition, not after.

Mistake Three: Overlooking How Assets Are Titled

How assets are titled matters as much as what they are worth.

Joint ownership, survivorship arrangements, and beneficiary designations can simplify or complicate estate settlement depending on jurisdiction. What works in Canada does not always translate cleanly in the United States.

Incorrect assumptions about titling can:

- Trigger unintended tax consequences
- Delay probate
- Create disputes among heirs

Mistake Four: Ignoring Liquidity Needs

Estate taxes and administrative costs often come due before assets can be sold or transferred.

Snowbirds with estates concentrated in property or long-term investments may leave heirs without the cash needed to meet obligations. This can force decisions that undermine long-term value.

Liquidity planning is not about excess. It is about timing.

Mistake Five: Treating Estate Planning as Static

Estate planning is often done once and filed away. For Snowbirds, that approach fails.

Travel patterns change. Assets are bought and sold. Laws evolve. What was appropriate five years ago may be inadequate today.

Cross-border estates require periodic review. Without it, plans slowly fall out of alignment with reality.

Why These Mistakes Persist

None of these mistakes come from recklessness. They come from complexity.

Snowbirds interact with multiple professionals, each focused on a specific area. Without coordination, gaps appear between advice.

The purpose of identifying these mistakes is not to assign fault. It is to make them visible while there is still time to correct them.

In the next section, we will look at **practical structures and strategies that reduce estate risk**, and how thoughtful planning can simplify outcomes for families on both sides of the border.

Planning Structures That Reduce Cross-Border Estate Risk

Once Snowbirds understand where estate exposure comes from, the next step is not panic. It is structure. Cross-border estate risk is rarely eliminated entirely, but it can be **reduced, contained, and made predictable** with thoughtful planning.

The goal is not complexity for its own sake. It is alignment.

Start With Coordinated Advice

Effective cross-border estate planning does not happen in isolation. It requires coordination between Canadian and U.S. professionals who understand how the systems interact.

When advisors work independently, solutions in one country can create problems in the other. When planning is coordinated, decisions reinforce each other instead of colliding.

Snowbirds benefit most when estate planning is approached as a cross-border exercise from the beginning, not retrofitted later.

Ownership Structure Matters

How assets are owned often determines how they are taxed and administered at death.

For U.S. real estate, ownership structure influences:

- Estate tax exposure
- Probate requirements
- Control over timing and disposition
- Administrative burden for heirs

No single structure works for everyone. What matters is understanding the trade-offs before committing to a form of ownership that is difficult to unwind later.

Separate Documents for Separate Jurisdictions

In some cases, maintaining separate wills or estate documents for Canadian and U.S. assets can reduce delays and confusion. This approach requires careful drafting to avoid overlap or conflict, but when done properly, it can streamline administration significantly.

The key is coordination, not duplication.

Plan for Liquidity, Not Just Taxes

Reducing tax exposure is only part of estate planning. Ensuring that estates have access to cash when obligations arise is equally important.

Liquidity planning allows heirs to:

- Pay taxes without forced sales
- Cover administrative costs
- Maintain flexibility in timing decisions

Without liquidity, even well-planned estates can experience unnecessary strain.

Review Plans as Your Snowbird Life Evolves

Snowbird life is not static. Travel patterns shift. Properties are bought and sold. Family circumstances change.

Estate plans should evolve alongside these changes. Regular review ensures that structures remain appropriate and that small adjustments prevent larger problems later.

The Value of Predictability

The most successful cross-border estate plans do not eliminate every obligation. They eliminate surprises.

Families know what to expect. Assets move on predictable timelines. Taxes are anticipated. Decisions are made deliberately rather than under pressure.

That predictability is the true measure of effective planning.

Looking Ahead: The Next Chapter

Chapter Seven explains how working while in the United States can create immigration and tax risk for Snowbirds, even when the employer and income are Canadian. It distinguishes the different questions immigration law and tax law ask, and clarifies what the U.S. treats as "work" regardless of intent or compensation. The chapter also explains how enforcement typically arises, why travel and activity patterns matter, and which types of professional behavior most commonly trigger border scrutiny. It closes with practical guidelines for staying engaged professionally while maintaining clear, defensible boundaries.

CHAPTER SEVEN
WORKING WHILE IN THE UNITED STATES: WHERE SNOWBIRDS CROSS THE LINE WITHOUT REALIZING IT

In This Chapter, You Will Learn...

In this chapter, you will learn how U.S. immigration and tax authorities evaluate work performed while physically present in the United States, and why well-intentioned Snowbirds often misunderstand where risk begins.

Specifically, this chapter will show you:

- Why working remotely from the U.S. can create problems even when the employer and income are Canadian
- How **immigration law and tax law ask different questions** and apply different standards
- What the United States actually considers "work," regardless of intent or compensation
- Why remote work, consulting, and family business involvement are frequently misclassified by Snowbirds

- How enforcement occurs in practice, and why patterns matter more than isolated actions
- The types of activities that tend to raise concerns at the border
- Practical ways to stay professionally engaged while maintaining clear, defensible boundaries

This chapter is designed to help Snowbirds understand where assumptions fail, where discretion applies, and how to preserve flexibility without unintentionally creating immigration or tax exposure.

"I'm Just Answering a Few Emails..."

This is the sentence that opens more difficult conversations than almost any other in the Snowbird world.

It usually comes from a place of honesty. People are not trying to bend rules or take advantage of loopholes. They are responding to a reality where work no longer requires an office, and where retirement no longer means disengagement. Laptops travel easily. Wi-Fi is everywhere. The boundary between working and not working feels thin.

The problem is that U.S. immigration and tax systems still rely on **physical presence**, not intention.

For Snowbirds, that gap between modern work habits and older legal frameworks creates real risk. A few emails, a handful of Zoom calls, or light involvement in a business can look harmless from a lifestyle perspective. From a regulatory perspective, those same actions can be interpreted very differently.

Why This Question Comes Up So Often Now

Snowbirds today are not the Snowbirds of twenty or thirty years ago. Many are semi-retired rather than fully retired. Some own businesses. Others consult, trade actively, or support family enterprises. Work is no longer something that stops when winter travel begins.

At the same time, border systems have become more data-driven. Officers look at patterns, not just answers. Tax authorities look at where services are performed, not just where income is paid. Assumptions that once went unchallenged now receive closer scrutiny.

This is why the question of working while in the U.S. matters more than ever.

Two Different Rulebooks Apply

One of the most important points to understand at the outset is that **two separate systems** govern this issue.

Immigration law asks whether you are allowed to perform work while physically present in the United States under the status you hold, usually visitor or Snowbird status.

Tax law asks whether income is taxable in the United States based on where services are performed, regardless of where the employer is located or where payment is deposited.

These systems operate independently. It is entirely possible to satisfy one while violating the other. It is also possible to run afoul of both at the same time.

This is where confusion takes root.

Why Assumptions Are Especially Dangerous Here

Many Snowbirds rely on informal logic. If the employer is Canadian, the work must be Canadian. If the income is paid into a Canadian account, it must be Canadian. If no U.S. clients are involved, there should be no U.S. issue.

None of those assumptions are reliable on their own.

What matters most, particularly from a U.S. perspective, is **where you are physically located when the work is performed**. That single factor influences both immigration interpretation and tax treatment.

This chapter exists because misunderstanding that point has led to denied entries, unexpected tax filings, employer complications, and long-term travel disruption for people who never believed they were doing anything risky.

In the sections that follow, we will separate what feels reasonable from what is actually permitted, examine where the grey areas exist, and outline practical guidelines Snowbirds can use to protect themselves.

Immigration Law and Tax Law: Two Separate Questions

One of the most persistent sources of confusion for Snowbirds who continue working while spending time in the United States is the assumption that immigration rules and tax rules are aligned. They are not.

These systems ask different questions, enforce different standards, and apply consequences in different ways. Understanding this distinction is essential, because compliance with one does not guarantee compliance with the other.

What Immigration Law Is Asking

U.S. immigration law is focused on **permission**.

When you enter the United States as a visitor, including under typical Snowbird travel patterns, you are granted permission to be present for a limited purpose and duration. That permission does not include authorization to work.

From an immigration perspective, the question is straightforward:

Are you performing activities that are considered work while physically present in the United States?

The answer does not depend on:

- Where your employer is located
- Where your clients reside
- Where your income is deposited
- Whether the work feels minimal or incidental

If the activity is classified as work, and you do not hold the appropriate authorization, you are out of status.

What Tax Law Is Asking

U.S. tax law is focused on **source**.

The IRS looks at where services are performed to determine where income is sourced. If you are physically present in the United States while performing services, the income associated with that work may be considered U.S.-source income.

This analysis does not depend on immigration status. Someone can violate immigration rules without creating a tax obligation, or create a tax obligation without triggering immediate immigration consequences. Often, however, the two overlap.

Why This Creates Risk for Snowbirds

Snowbirds often assume that small amounts of work fall below a meaningful threshold. They do not.

Immigration law does not provide a safe harbor for limited hours, volunteer-style involvement, or informal participation. Tax law does not ignore income simply because it was modest or infrequent.

The danger lies in visibility. Once work is acknowledged, documented, or questioned, it becomes difficult to explain away after the fact.

Why Intent Does Not Control the Outcome

Snowbirds rarely intend to work illegally or create tax exposure. Intent, however, is not the deciding factor.

Both immigration and tax systems rely on **objective facts**:

- Where you were
- What you did
- When you did it

Good faith explanations matter less than documentation.

The Structural Mismatch

The modern reality of remote work has outpaced the structure of the rules that govern it. Snowbirds live in that gap. What feels normal in daily life may still fall outside what is permitted under existing frameworks.

This is why understanding both rulebooks is critical. You cannot manage risk if you are reading only one.

In the next section, we will look at **what the U.S. considers "work"**, and why that definition is broader than many Snowbirds expect.

What the United States Considers "Work"

Most Snowbirds are surprised to learn that the U.S. definition of work is far broader than they expect. That surprise usually comes from assuming that work must be formal, paid, or visible to qualify. Under U.S. rules, none of those assumptions hold.

From both an immigration and tax perspective, **work is defined by activity, not intention**.

Work Is About Services, Not Pay

A common misconception is that if no money is earned in the United States, no work is taking place. That is not how the system operates.

Work includes:

- Performing services
- Contributing labour or expertise
- Supporting a business or organization
- Advancing commercial activity

Payment is not required. Compensation can be indirect, deferred, or tied to future outcomes. Even unpaid involvement can still be classified as work if it benefits a business or organization.

Remote Work Is Still Work

Remote work does not avoid scrutiny simply because it is digital.

If you are:

- Attending meetings
- Writing reports
- Managing employees
- Providing advice
- Making decisions
- Trading actively as part of a business

and you are physically present in the United States while doing so, that activity may be considered work performed in the U.S.

The fact that clients, employers, or servers are located elsewhere does not change where the work occurred.

"It's Just a Few Hours" Is Not a Defense

There is no minimum number of hours that makes work permissible under visitor status.

A single meeting can qualify.
An occasional task can qualify.
Ongoing low-level involvement can qualify.

Snowbirds often believe that scale determines compliance. In reality, **classification does**.

Volunteer and Family Business Involvement

Another area of misunderstanding involves volunteering or helping family businesses.

Volunteer work for organizations that would normally pay for services can be considered unauthorized employment. Helping a family member manage a business, even informally, can still be viewed as work if it contributes to operations or revenue.

The personal nature of the relationship does not override the activity itself.

Why This Line Is So Easy to Cross

Modern work habits blur boundaries. Devices are portable. Communication is constant. People remain engaged without feeling like they are "working."

U.S. rules, however, have not adapted to these changes. They still draw lines based on presence and activity, not lifestyle.

This disconnect is why Snowbirds often cross the line unintentionally.

Why Consistency Matters

Occasional incidental activity is sometimes overlooked. Repeated, patterned activity is not.

When work becomes routine, predictable, or tied to extended stays, it becomes easier for authorities to identify and harder to explain away.

Understanding what qualifies as work is not about avoiding productivity. It is about avoiding unintended consequences.

In the next section, we will look at **how these rules are enforced in real life**, and why some Snowbirds are questioned while others are not.

How These Rules Are Enforced in Practice

Snowbirds often ask the same question once they understand the rules:

"If this is such a risk, why don't more people get caught?"

The answer is not reassuring, but it is important. Enforcement is **selective, situational, and cumulative**. Most people are not flagged because a single action rarely triggers scrutiny on its own. Problems arise when activities intersect with visibility, patterns, or questioning.

The Border Is the First Point of Exposure

For most Snowbirds, enforcement begins at the border, not behind a desk.

Customs and Border Protection officers are trained to assess intent. They do this by listening to answers, reviewing travel history, and looking for inconsistencies between what a traveler says and what their pattern suggests.

Work-related issues often surface when:

- Travel is frequent or extended
- Stays are consistent year after year
- Ownership of U.S. property is involved
- Answers feel rehearsed or incomplete
- Devices or documentation raise questions

An officer does not need proof of employment to ask questions. They need a reason to probe further.

Admissions Matter More Than Evidence

One of the most common ways Snowbirds create problems for themselves is through **casual admissions**.

Statements like:

- "I check in with the office now and then"
- "I'm semi-retired"
- "I still help out a bit"

- "I run things remotely"

may feel harmless. In an immigration context, they can open a line of questioning that is difficult to close.

Once work is acknowledged, the burden shifts to the traveler to explain why that activity is permitted. That is rarely a comfortable position.

Patterns Are More Important Than Incidents

Authorities are far more interested in patterns than isolated moments.

Someone who answers a single email once is unlikely to draw attention. Someone who spends months in the U.S. every year while remaining professionally active creates a profile that invites questions.

Patterns develop quietly. They are rarely noticed by the person living them.

Tax Enforcement Often Comes Later

Tax consequences, when they arise, often do so well after the activity occurred.

Information can surface through:

- Employer reporting
- Cross-border audits
- Banking or investment disclosures
- Inconsistencies between filings

By the time tax issues emerge, the activity is already documented. Explanations become retrospective rather than preventive.

Why Enforcement Feels Inconsistent

Snowbirds often compare stories. One person works quietly for years without issue. Another is questioned immediately.

This inconsistency is not randomness. It reflects differences in:

- Travel frequency
- Length of stays
- Transparency of activity
- Prior questioning or notations
- How explanations are delivered

Enforcement is not designed to catch everyone. It is designed to address situations that rise above a threshold of concern.

The Risk Is Not Punishment. It Is Disruption

The most common consequences are not dramatic penalties. They are disruptions.

Shortened entries.
Increased questioning.
Notations on files.
Future scrutiny.
Forced changes to travel patterns.

These outcomes affect quality of life long before they affect finances.

In the next section, we will look at **how Snowbirds can remain engaged professionally without creating unnecessary risk**, and what practical boundaries help preserve flexibility.

Staying Engaged Without Creating Problems

For many Snowbirds, the goal is not to stop being useful, curious, or connected. It is to avoid crossing lines they never intended to approach in the first place.

The challenge lies in recognizing that engagement and work are not the same thing under U.S. rules, even when they feel similar in daily life.

Why Boundaries Matter More Than Labels

Snowbirds often describe themselves as semi-retired, consultants, advisors, or business owners who are "mostly inactive." These labels may be accurate in a personal sense. They do not control how activity is interpreted.

What matters is not how you describe your role, but **what you actually do while physically present in the United States**.

Clear boundaries reduce ambiguity. Ambiguity invites scrutiny.

Activities That Typically Carry Less Risk

Certain activities are generally less likely to raise concerns when done occasionally and without compensation tied to U.S. presence. These include:

- Passive investment monitoring
- Educational reading or professional development
- High-level strategic thinking not tied to execution
- Maintaining personal relationships unrelated to business operations

These activities do not advance commercial outcomes directly and are easier to distinguish from active service.

Activities That Deserve Caution

Other activities deserve careful thought because they resemble service delivery:

- Participating in operational meetings
- Managing employees or contractors
- Producing work product
- Negotiating contracts
- Representing a business externally

When these actions occur repeatedly during U.S. stays, they are harder to separate from work performed in the United States.

The Importance of Consistency

One-off activity may pass unnoticed. Repetition changes perception.

Snowbirds who engage professionally while in the U.S. often underestimate how patterns develop. Consistency is easier to see from the outside than from within.

This is why discipline matters more than justification.

Why Transparency Must Be Strategic

Honesty is essential. Oversharing is not.

Snowbirds sometimes volunteer information at the border in an effort to appear cooperative. Unfortunately, vague or casual explanations can create more questions than they answer.

Clear, concise responses grounded in accurate understanding are far more effective than improvised explanations.

When Professional Advice Becomes Necessary

If your situation involves ongoing business ownership, consulting arrangements, or income-producing activity that does not pause during U.S. stays, professional advice is not optional.

The cost of clarity is almost always lower than the cost of correction.

The Core Principle

The safest approach is not withdrawal. It is **intentional separation**.

When Snowbirds understand how work is defined, how patterns are evaluated, and how enforcement occurs, they can make informed decisions that preserve flexibility without abandoning engagement.

That awareness is the real protection.

Looking Ahead: The Next Chapter

Chapter Eight explains how Canadian residency is evaluated for Snowbirds living part-time outside the country. It outlines the primary and secondary ties Canada considers, why physical presence alone does not determine status, and how residency can weaken gradually through travel, financial, and lifestyle patterns. The chapter also examines the role of provincial health coverage as an indicator of residency strength and provides practical steps to reinforce Canadian residency while maintaining cross-border flexibility.

CHAPTER EIGHT
MAINTAINING CANADIAN RESIDENCY WHILE LIVING A CROSS-BORDER LIFE

In This Chapter, You Will Learn...

This chapter focuses on what it actually means to **remain Canadian** while spending meaningful time outside the country, and why residency is shaped by patterns, not single decisions.

In this chapter, you will learn:

- How Canadian residency is evaluated across tax, healthcare, and administrative systems
- Why physical presence alone does not determine residency
- The role of housing, finances, family ties, and community connections in residency decisions
- How provincial health coverage acts as an early signal of residency strength or weakness
- Why residency erosion often happens gradually, without obvious warning signs
- How travel habits and lifestyle choices affect long-term status
- Practical ways to reinforce Canadian residency while maintaining flexibility abroad

This chapter is designed to help Snowbirds recognize residency as an **ongoing practice**, not a one-time determination, and to understand how reinforcing it consistently protects both freedom of movement and long-term stability.

Why Canadian Residency Is the Anchor of Snowbird Life

For many Snowbirds, Canadian residency is something they assume rather than actively maintain. Taxes are filed. Health cards are renewed. A home remains in Canada. On the surface, nothing appears to have changed.

In reality, residency is not a static label. It is a status that is evaluated continuously, often indirectly, based on patterns, ties, and behavior over time.

This chapter begins here because **Canadian residency underpins almost every other cross-border outcome**. Tax obligations, healthcare eligibility, estate exposure, and even how U.S. authorities view your travel all trace back to whether Canada continues to see you as a resident.

Residency Is About Facts, Not Declarations

Snowbirds sometimes believe residency is determined by intention or by a single action, such as filing a tax return or keeping a mailing address. Canadian authorities do not evaluate residency that way.

Residency is assessed based on **the totality of your ties**. No single factor controls the outcome. Instead, patterns are reviewed collectively.

What matters is not what you believe your status to be, but whether your life still looks Canadian when viewed from the outside.

Why This Becomes Riskier Over Time

Residency erosion rarely happens in a single year. It occurs gradually.

Longer absences.
Reduced time at a Canadian home.
Increased reliance on U.S. services.
Stronger personal routines outside Canada.

Each change feels reasonable on its own. Together, they can shift how residency is interpreted.

Snowbirds often discover this shift only when something triggers review, such as a healthcare claim, a tax inquiry, or a change in filing status.

The Cost of Losing Residency Is Often Underestimated

Losing Canadian residency is not simply a tax classification change. It can affect:

- Eligibility for provincial health coverage
- Access to certain benefits and credits
- How assets are taxed
- How future returns to Canada are treated

In some cases, regaining residency can be difficult and time-consuming.

This is why residency should be managed deliberately, not assumed.

Why This Chapter Matters Now

Earlier chapters addressed how U.S. systems evaluate presence, work, healthcare, property, and estates. This chapter brings the focus home.

Understanding how Canada views your life is essential to managing how both countries interact with you. Residency is the anchor point that keeps the rest of your planning aligned.

In the sections that follow, we will examine:

- How Canada defines residency
- Which ties matter most
- How Snowbirds unintentionally weaken those ties
- Practical ways to maintain residency while living part-time abroad

This is not about limiting your Snowbird lifestyle. It is about protecting the foundation that allows it to continue.

How Canada Determines Residency

Canadian residency is not decided by a single rule or form. It is assessed by reviewing **how your life is structured**, not by how you describe it. This distinction matters, because many Snowbirds believe residency is preserved through one or two actions, when in fact it is the overall pattern that controls the outcome.

Canadian authorities look at residency as a question of **connection**.

Primary Residential Ties

At the center of residency analysis are primary residential ties. These carry the greatest weight and are often decisive.

Primary ties include:

- A dwelling place available for your use in Canada
- A spouse or partner residing in Canada
- Dependents who remain in Canada

These ties indicate where your personal life is anchored. Weakening or severing them without understanding the consequences is one of the fastest ways Snowbirds unintentionally put residency at risk.

Secondary Residential Ties

Secondary ties do not usually determine residency on their own, but they reinforce the picture created by primary ties. Over time, erosion across many secondary ties can shift how residency is viewed.

Secondary ties include:

- Canadian bank accounts and credit cards
- Provincial health coverage
- Driver's licence and vehicle registration
- Social memberships and professional affiliations
- Canadian mailing address
- Filing Canadian tax returns

No single secondary tie is decisive. Their strength lies in accumulation.

Why Presence Alone Is Not Enough

Some Snowbirds believe that spending a minimum number of days in Canada each year guarantees residency. That belief is unreliable.

Physical presence matters, but it is evaluated alongside other ties. A person can spend time in Canada and still be considered a non-resident if other connections have weakened sufficiently.

Conversely, someone can spend significant time abroad and remain a Canadian resident if ties remain strong and consistent.

Why Canada Looks at the Big Picture

Residency determinations are rarely triggered without cause. Reviews often follow:

- Extended absences
- Changes in tax filings
- Loss of provincial health coverage
- Asset restructuring
- Requests for benefits

When a review occurs, authorities do not rely on snapshots. They examine history.

This is why Snowbirds should think in terms of **patterns**, not thresholds.

The Snowbird Trap

Snowbirds often manage U.S. exposure carefully while assuming Canadian residency will take care of itself. This imbalance creates risk.

Maintaining Canadian residency requires active attention, particularly when time spent outside the country increases.

In the next section, we will look at **how Snowbirds unintentionally weaken residency**, and which behaviors deserve closer scrutiny before they accumulate into a problem.

How Snowbirds Unintentionally Weaken Canadian Residency

Most Snowbirds do not set out to abandon Canadian residency. When it is lost or questioned, it is almost always the result of **small, reasonable decisions made repeatedly over time**.

The risk does not come from one action. It comes from accumulation.

Spending More Time Away Without Rebalancing Ties

Extended time outside Canada does not automatically end residency, but it does increase scrutiny. When long absences are not balanced by strong, ongoing ties at home, residency begins to look less stable.

Snowbirds often focus on managing U.S. day limits while overlooking how reduced presence in Canada affects the overall picture. Over time, Canada may no longer appear to be the center of day-to-day life.

Letting a Canadian Home Become Passive

Owning property in Canada is helpful only if it remains meaningfully connected to your life.

A home that is rented long-term, rarely occupied, or treated as an investment rather than a residence carries less weight than many Snowbirds assume. Availability matters. Use matters.

A Canadian residence should look like a place you live, not simply a property you own.

Eroding Health Coverage Without Realizing It

Provincial health coverage is one of the clearest indicators of residency. Losing coverage, suspending it, or allowing eligibility to lapse sends a strong signal.

Snowbirds often discover the issue only after returning to Canada and needing care. At that point, reinstatement can be slow and conditional.

Health coverage loss is rarely decisive on its own, but it significantly weakens the residency profile.

Shifting Financial Life Elsewhere

Opening U.S. accounts, using U.S. financial services more frequently, or relying on foreign institutions for daily transactions can subtly shift where your financial life appears to be centered.

This does not mean Snowbirds should avoid necessary accounts. It means Canadian accounts should remain active and clearly connected to regular life.

Downplaying Social and Community Ties

Social connections may feel informal, but they matter.

Clubs, memberships, professional affiliations, and community involvement contribute to the overall picture of where life is anchored. When these ties fade without replacement, residency becomes easier to question.

Why These Changes Feel Harmless

Each of these adjustments feels practical in isolation. Together, they create a pattern that suggests transition rather than temporary absence.

Snowbirds often assume residency is preserved until explicitly revoked. In reality, residency is assessed when questions arise, based on the pattern already established.

In the next section, we will look at **practical steps Snowbirds can take to reinforce Canadian residency**, even while spending significant time abroad.

Reinforcing Canadian Residency While Living Part-Time Abroad

Maintaining Canadian residency does not require constant presence, but it does require **intentional structure**. Snowbirds who preserve residency successfully are not those who restrict their travel most, but those who ensure their lives continue to look Canadian when viewed as a whole.

The goal is continuity, not rigidity.

Keep Your Canadian Home Central to Your Life

A Canadian residence should remain more than a mailing address. Availability and use matter.

Returning regularly, maintaining utilities, and treating the home as a true base reinforces the idea that Canada remains your primary place of living, even if you spend extended periods elsewhere. A residence that feels lived in carries more weight than one that exists only on paper.

Protect Provincial Health Coverage

Provincial health coverage is one of the strongest indicators of residency. Snowbirds should understand their province's absence limits and plan travel accordingly.

Maintaining coverage involves more than avoiding cancellation. It means meeting physical presence requirements and ensuring documentation is current. Once coverage is lost, reinstatement can be slow and conditional.

Health coverage is not just a benefit. It is evidence.

Anchor Financial and Administrative Life in Canada

Canadian bank accounts, credit cards, and investment relationships should remain active and relevant. Filing Canadian tax returns consistently, using Canadian professionals, and maintaining a Canadian mailing address reinforce residency.

Shifting too many day-to-day functions elsewhere weakens the overall profile, even when done for convenience.

Maintain Social and Community Connections

Residency is about life, not just assets.

Community involvement, family relationships, memberships, and professional ties help demonstrate where your personal world is centered. These connections do not need to be formal, but they should be real and ongoing.

Balance Travel With Visibility at Home

Snowbirds often manage U.S. exposure carefully while assuming Canadian presence will take care of itself. The opposite approach is more effective.

Being visible in Canada at meaningful intervals, rather than minimizing time there, strengthens residency more reliably than strict day-count strategies alone.

Residency as an Ongoing Practice

Residency is not something you establish once. It is something you maintain.

Snowbirds who revisit their residency profile periodically, especially as travel patterns or personal circumstances change, are better positioned to address issues early rather than respond to them later.

In the next section, we will bring these concepts together and look at **how residency interacts with taxation, healthcare, and long-term planning**, and why alignment across systems matters.

When Residency, Tax, and Lifestyle Decisions Collide

Most Snowbirds encounter problems not because they misunderstand a single rule, but because they treat each system in isolation. Residency, taxation, healthcare eligibility, and immigration status do not operate independently in real life.

They intersect through your behavior, your travel patterns, and the choices you make year after year.

This is where complexity quietly accumulates.

Residency Is the Anchor Point

Canadian residency sits at the center of the Snowbird experience. It influences how taxes are assessed, whether provincial health coverage continues, and how authorities interpret your intent when you cross borders.

Weakening residency does not always trigger immediate consequences. Often, the impact appears later, when you file a return, apply for coverage, or are asked to explain a pattern that developed over time.

Tax Consequences Follow Patterns, Not Intentions

Tax authorities respond to cumulative behavior. Spending more time outside Canada, relying on foreign property, or shifting financial routines abroad can gradually change how your situation is viewed.

Snowbirds who assume that filing Canadian taxes alone secures residency often discover that other factors are weighed just as heavily. The structure of your life matters as much as where income is reported.

Healthcare Eligibility Reflects Physical Presence

Provincial health plans rely on presence thresholds and residency indicators that do not align neatly with tax or immigration rules. Losing coverage is often the first visible signal that residency has been weakened, even when taxes remain unchanged.

Once coverage lapses, restoring it can involve waiting periods, documentation, and conditions that affect travel plans and peace of mind.

Lifestyle Choices Carry Administrative Weight

Seemingly personal decisions often carry administrative consequences. Long annual absences, consistent extended stays abroad, or shifting daily routines outside Canada can alter how authorities interpret your primary residence.

Snowbirds who plan with awareness understand that lifestyle flexibility increases when decisions are aligned across systems, not when one area is optimized at the expense of another.

Alignment Creates Stability

The most stable Snowbird arrangements share a common feature: alignment.

Travel patterns support tax planning. Residency supports healthcare eligibility. Financial routines reflect where life is centered. Immigration behavior matches visitor status.

When these elements reinforce one another, compliance becomes easier and surprises are rare.

Planning Ahead Reduces Friction Later

Snowbirds who reassess their situation periodically, especially after changes in travel, property ownership, or family circumstances, maintain control over outcomes. Those who wait until a problem surfaces often find fewer options available.

This chapter closes with a central principle: cross-border living works best when decisions are made with a full view of the system, not just the part immediately in front of you.

Looking Ahead: The Next Chapter

Chapter Nine examines the Snowbird Act and explains what it proposes, why it continues to stall, and why it should not shape day-to-day planning until it becomes law. It clarifies that extended visitor time would not alter U.S. tax residency rules, Canadian residency requirements, or healthcare eligibility. The chapter also explains why longer stays could increase planning complexity rather than reduce it, and why accurate day tracking remains essential under current law. It concludes by outlining how structured recordkeeping and informed interpretation support disciplined cross-border planning during legislative uncertainty.

CHAPTER NINE
THE SNOWBIRD ACT: SEPARATING HOPE, HEADLINES, AND REALITY

This chapter examines the Snowbird Act through a practical planning lens, helping Snowbirds understand what the proposal does, why it continues to resurface, and why it should not shape day-to-day decisions until it becomes law.

In this chapter, you will learn:

- What the Snowbird Act is designed to change — and what it does not address
- Why repeated reintroduction of the bill does not signal imminent reform
- How immigration permission, tax residency, and Canadian residency operate independently
- Why longer stays would increase planning complexity rather than reduce it
- How to think about proposed legislation without letting it distort real-world choices
- Why accurate day tracking remains essential regardless of policy outcomes
- How the Snowbirds U.S. Day Tracker™ App supports disciplined planning under current law

- The role of the Snowbirds Expat Radio Podcast in interpreting evolving rules and enforcement

This chapter is intended to replace speculation with clarity, allowing Snowbirds to stay informed without relying on assumptions, and to plan confidently within the rules that apply today.

The Snowbird Act: What It Promises, What It Doesn't, and Why It Matters

For many Canadian Snowbirds, no topic generates more hope, speculation, and confusion than the so-called Snowbird Act. The idea is simple and appealing: more time in the United States without triggering immigration or tax problems. Eight months instead of six. Fewer forced returns. A lifestyle that better reflects how retirees actually live today.

That hope resurfaces every few years when headlines announce that the bill has been "reintroduced." Conversations light up in RV parks, condo associations, golf courses, and online forums. Some people begin planning around the assumption that change is imminent.

This chapter exists to slow that momentum down and replace it with clarity.

The Snowbird Act is not law. It has never been law. And despite repeated introductions in Congress, it remains a proposal with significant structural obstacles standing in its way. Understanding what the bill actually contains, why it continues to stall, and how it fits into the existing cross-border framework is essential for Snowbirds who want to plan responsibly rather than react to headlines.

What the Snowbird Act Is Designed to Do

At its core, the Snowbird Act attempts to address a real demographic shift. Canadians are living longer, remaining active later in life, and spending more time in the United States during the winter months. The existing six-month limit, while workable, often feels misaligned with modern retirement patterns.

The proposed legislation seeks to extend the maximum period Canadians can remain in the U.S. as visitors from roughly six months to approximately eight months per year. The intent is narrow. It does not offer a pathway to U.S. residency. It does not grant work authorization. It does not eliminate tax rules. It simply proposes additional visitor time for a specific population under defined conditions.

That distinction is important, because much of the confusion surrounding the bill comes from assumptions about what longer stays would automatically permit. They would not.

- The Snowbird Act is a **proposed bill**, not law
- It does **not** grant U.S. residency or work authorization
- It does **not** change U.S. tax residency rules
- It does **not** override Canadian residency or healthcare requirements
- It only addresses **length of visitor stays**, under specific conditions

Why the Bill Sounds Simple but Isn't

From a Snowbird's perspective, the request seems reasonable. More time to enjoy property already owned. More flexibility to avoid winter travel. Greater continuity in seasonal living.

From a policy perspective, however, the bill intersects with multiple systems that were never designed to operate independently. Immigration limits, tax residency rules, enforcement mechanisms, and data tracking would all be affected by an extended stay allowance.

This is where resistance emerges.

Extending visitor stays without altering tax residency thresholds creates tension with existing IRS rules. Allowing longer stays without enhanced monitoring raises enforcement concerns. Preserving non-resident tax status while increasing physical presence challenges longstanding policy assumptions.

None of these issues are insurmountable, but they explain why the bill has struggled to gain momentum despite repeated introductions.

The Current Reality Snowbirds Must Plan Around

As of now, the Snowbird Act remains proposed legislation only. No version has advanced far enough to produce meaningful change. No timeline exists. No implementation framework has been approved. Snowbirds planning travel today must operate under the rules currently in force, not those that may exist someday.

This chapter will walk through what the most recent version of the bill proposes, why it continues to stall, and what Snowbirds should realistically expect going forward. The goal is not to dismiss the idea, but to place it in proper context so decisions are based on facts rather than optimism.

Planning around existing rules is not pessimism. It is prudence.

Where the Snowbird Act Actually Stands

One of the most persistent misunderstandings surrounding the Snowbird Act is the belief that reintroduction equals progress. Each time the bill appears again in Congress, it is often described as "back on the table," creating the impression that change is imminent.

In practice, legislative reintroduction is often procedural, not predictive.

Why Reintroduction Is Not Momentum

Bills that fail to advance during a congressional session do not carry forward automatically. They must be reintroduced in subsequent sessions to remain alive at all. This is common, especially for proposals that address niche populations rather than broad national priorities.

The Snowbird Act has followed this pattern. It is periodically reintroduced, referred to committee, and then stalls. The absence of debate, amendment, or floor scheduling indicates limited legislative urgency, not quiet progress.

- Bills must be reintroduced each congressional session
- Reintroduction does **not** indicate increased likelihood of passage
- Committee review is often where bills stall
- Lack of floor debate signals low legislative priority

The Committees That Control Its Fate

For the Snowbird Act to advance, it must pass through committees that oversee immigration and border policy. These committees are tasked with balancing national security, enforcement capacity, and immigration integrity.

Visitor extensions, even for a narrow group like Canadian Snowbirds, raise questions about monitoring, compliance, and precedent. These concerns tend to slow momentum long before public debate begins.

Why Political Support Remains Fragile

The bill enjoys intermittent bipartisan interest, often driven by border-state tourism economies and constituent advocacy. However, this support tends to be shallow.

Extended visitor stays compete with broader immigration priorities, enforcement debates, and border security initiatives. In that environment, a bill designed for seasonal retirees rarely rises to the top of the agenda.

Why Snowbirds Keep Hearing About It Anyway

Media coverage and advocacy efforts play a significant role in keeping the Snowbird Act visible. Each reintroduction becomes newsworthy within Snowbird communities, even when legislative prospects remain unchanged.

This repetition creates a cycle of hope followed by disappointment, particularly for those who interpret visibility as inevitability.

What This Means for Planning

The legislative process moves slowly, and change is rarely linear. Snowbirds who plan as if the Snowbird Act will pass risk building assumptions into travel, tax, and residency decisions that are not supported by current law.

Until enacted, the bill has no legal effect. Immigration limits, tax rules, and enforcement practices remain exactly as they are today.

In the next section, we will examine **why even if the Snowbird Act were to pass, it would not resolve many of the core risks Snowbirds face**, particularly around taxation and residency.

Why More Time Would Not Mean Fewer Rules

Even if the Snowbird Act were enacted exactly as proposed, it would not simplify cross-border life in the way many people expect. In some respects, it could make planning more complex rather than less.

The reason is straightforward. **Time in the United States affects more than immigration status.** Extending visitor stays does not suspend tax rules, residency tests, or compliance obligations that are triggered by physical presence.

- Immigration permission ≠ tax residency safety
- Longer stays increase visibility, not protection
- IRS Substantial Presence Test remains unchanged
- Provincial health rules do not adjust automatically
- Canadian residency erosion can accelerate

Immigration Permission Does Not Equal Tax Safety

Immigration law and tax law operate independently. A person can be lawfully present in the United States and still create tax residency exposure.

The Snowbird Act, as proposed, focuses only on visitor duration. It does not modify the IRS Substantial Presence Test. It does not change reporting thresholds. It does not alter how the IRS evaluates cumulative presence.

Snowbirds who assume longer permitted stays would reduce tax risk misunderstand the separation between these systems.

Longer Stays Increase Visibility

Extended presence increases patterns. Patterns increase scrutiny.

Spending eight months in the U.S. every year would make travel histories more consistent, more predictable, and more visible to both immigration and tax authorities. While lawful, such consistency can invite deeper examination of intent, ties, and activity.

The Snowbird Act would not insulate travelers from that reality.

Healthcare and Residency Consequences Remain

Canadian provincial health plans rely on physical presence and residency indicators that are unaffected by U.S. immigration allowances. Longer stays south of the border could accelerate loss of coverage unless travel is carefully managed.

Similarly, Canadian tax residency is shaped by ties and presence over time. Longer absences can weaken those ties even if immigration rules permit extended stays.

The Planning Burden Would Increase, Not Decrease

Paradoxically, additional flexibility often requires more discipline.

Snowbirds permitted to remain longer in the U.S. would need tighter tracking, clearer boundaries around work, stronger documentation of Canadian ties, and more deliberate health coverage planning.

The margin for error would shrink, not expand.

Why This Matters Now

Believing that future legislative change will simplify planning encourages delay. Delay increases risk.

Snowbirds who understand that more time does not eliminate complexity are better positioned to plan under existing rules and adapt if changes eventually occur.

In the next section, we will look at **how Snowbirds should think about proposed legislation without letting it distort real-world decision-making**.

How Snowbirds Should Treat Proposed Legislation

Hope is not a strategy.

Proposed legislation can be useful as a signal of long-term direction, but it should never become the foundation for personal planning. The Snowbird Act illustrates this clearly. Its repeated reintroduction shows awareness of a demographic reality, but awareness does not guarantee action.

Snowbirds who stay grounded understand the difference.

- Plan under current law
- Treat proposals as context, not permission
- Avoid delaying necessary adjustments
- Preserve flexibility through compliance

Proposals Reflect Discussion, Not Permission

A bill represents conversation, not authority. Until it becomes law, it carries no legal weight and provides no protection at the border, with the IRS, or with Canadian authorities.

Planning based on what a bill *might* allow creates exposure because enforcement decisions are made based on current law, not future intent.

Why Waiting Can Create Risk

Some Snowbirds delay adjustments to travel patterns, tax filings, or residency planning because they believe relief is coming. That delay can be costly.

Travel days accumulate regardless of legislative headlines. Residency ties erode quietly. Health coverage requirements do not pause while Congress debates.

The systems continue to operate even when reform is discussed.

Greater Risk of Triggering U.S. Tax Residency

Even with exemptions, Canadians could inadvertently expose themselves to:

- U.S. income tax
- U.S. estate tax
- State income tax
- Loss of treaty protection

More Scrutiny From DHS, IRS, and CBP

Longer stays likely mean more tracking, more verification, and greater administrative complexity.

Use Proposed Laws as Context, Not Direction

Proposed legislation can help Snowbirds understand how policymakers are thinking about long-term trends. It can inform advocacy and future expectations.

It should not dictate travel schedules, property decisions, or tax strategy.

The safest approach is to remain compliant under current rules while staying informed about possible changes.

Flexibility Comes From Planning, Not Permission

Snowbirds who plan conservatively retain options. Those who assume flexibility will be granted later often find themselves constrained.

Planning under existing law allows Snowbirds to adapt smoothly if changes occur. Planning ahead of the law removes that margin.

The Responsible Position

Acknowledging the Snowbird Act without relying on it is not pessimism. It is disciplined planning.

Snowbirds who respect the boundaries of current law are better prepared for whatever reforms eventually arrive, whether they expand flexibility or not.

In the next section, we will close the chapter by summarizing what the Snowbird Act means for Snowbirds today, and what it does not.

What the Snowbird Act Means for You Today

The Snowbird Act continues to capture attention because it speaks to a real frustration. The current system does not always align neatly with how Snowbirds live. Longer stays feel reasonable. Seasonal routines feel settled. The desire for flexibility is understandable.

What matters, however, is separating **possibility from reality**.

As things stand, the Snowbird Act changes nothing about how Snowbirds must plan their lives today. Immigration limits remain in place. Tax residency rules continue to apply. Canadian healthcare and residency requirements are unchanged. Every system Snowbirds interact with still evaluates behavior based on existing law.

Why This Chapter Exists

This chapter is not meant to discourage interest in legislative reform. It exists to prevent false confidence.

Snowbirds who understand the limits of proposed legislation are less likely to make assumptions that create downstream problems. They recognize that policy discussions do not suspend enforcement, and that compliance today preserves flexibility tomorrow.

How the Snowbirds U.S. Day Tracker™ App Protects Canadians — With or Without This Bill

One of the reasons the Snowbird Act generates so much attention is uncertainty. When rules feel unstable or subject to change, people look for something dependable to anchor their decisions. That is where disciplined tracking becomes essential.

Regardless of whether the Snowbird Act ever passes, the systems that currently govern Snowbird life continue to operate. Immigration limits, tax residency rules, and enforcement practices all rely on **documented presence**, not assumptions or intent. In that environment, accurate records matter more than optimism.

The Snowbirds U.S. Day Tracker™ App was built to address that reality, not to anticipate legislative reform.

- Interpretation of rule changes
- Context behind enforcement trends
- Expert perspectives across disciplines
- Clarification during legislative uncertainty

What the App Actually Does — and Why That Matters

The app does not attempt to predict policy outcomes or replace professional advice. Its role is narrower and more practical: it helps Snowbirds maintain **clear, defensible records** of their time in the United States.

Specifically, the app allows users to:

- Manually enter U.S. entry and exit dates with precision
- View cumulative U.S. days calculated according to IRS methodology
- Monitor rolling multi-year totals rather than single calendar years
- Identify when travel patterns begin to approach risk thresholds

This structure is intentional. Many Snowbirds limit mobile data use while in the U.S., and not all users want location-based tracking. Manual entry keeps the system reliable, transparent, and under the user's control.

Why Manual Tracking Is Not a Weakness

Some people assume automation is safer. In cross-border planning, **accuracy and accountability** matter more than convenience.

Manual entry:

- Forces awareness of travel patterns
- Creates a deliberate habit of review
- Produces records that can be explained and supported if questioned

In situations involving tax residency or border scrutiny, being able to explain *how* your days were tracked can be just as important as the numbers themselves.

Protection That Does Not Depend on Policy Change

If the Snowbird Act never passes, the app remains relevant because:

- The IRS Substantial Presence Test remains unchanged
- Canadian residency evaluations continue to rely on presence patterns
- Border questioning still depends on travel history

If the Snowbird Act were ever enacted, the app would remain relevant because:

- Tax residency rules would still apply

- Longer stays would increase the importance of cumulative tracking
- Visibility and consistency would matter even more

In both scenarios, the underlying risk does not disappear. It simply shifts.

Key Point for Snowbirds

- Legislative proposals do not protect you
- Assumptions do not protect you
- Accurate records do

The Snowbirds U.S. Day Tracker™ App exists to provide structure in an environment where certainty is limited. It does not eliminate rules, but it helps Snowbirds live within them deliberately rather than reactively.

Snowbirds Expat Radio Podcast: Staying Informed When the Rules Don't Stand Still

One of the challenges of cross-border planning is that rules do not remain static. Immigration practices evolve. Tax enforcement priorities shift. Administrative interpretations change quietly, often without public announcement. A book can provide structure and grounding, but it cannot update itself.

That reality is why ongoing education matters just as much as foundational understanding.

The Snowbirds Expat Radio Podcast was created to fill that gap. Its purpose is not to replace professional advice or provide shortcuts. It exists to help Snowbirds stay oriented in a system where clarity often arrives late and misinformation spreads quickly.

Why Static Information Isn't Enough

Many Snowbirds rely on advice they heard years ago. Others follow headlines without context. Both approaches create risk.

Rules change in ways that are:

- Incremental rather than dramatic
- Interpreted differently by different authorities
- Applied unevenly depending on facts and patterns

Without reliable interpretation, Snowbirds are left reacting instead of planning.

What the Podcast Provides

The podcast brings together professionals who work directly within the systems Snowbirds encounter. Immigration lawyers, cross-border accountants, tax specialists, healthcare experts, and planners explain not only what the rules are, but how they are applied in practice.

Listeners gain insight into:

- How enforcement actually unfolds
- Where common assumptions fail
- Which changes matter immediately and which do not
- How individual choices interact with broader policy

This context is especially important during periods of legislative uncertainty, such as ongoing discussion around the Snowbird Act.

Why This Matters During Policy Debate

When proposed legislation attracts attention, interpretation becomes more important than headlines. The podcast provides a way to understand:

- What a proposal does and does not change
- How existing rules continue to apply
- Why waiting for reform can create unintended exposure

Rather than encouraging speculation, the focus remains on operating safely under current law while staying informed about potential developments.

A Complement to the Book, Not a Substitute

This book is designed to give Snowbirds a structured understanding of the cross-border landscape. The podcast extends that understanding over time.

Together, they serve different roles:

- The book establishes foundational principles
- The podcast provides ongoing interpretation
- The app supports disciplined recordkeeping

Each element addresses a different aspect of the same problem: living well across borders without relying on assumptions.

The Real Takeaway

The Snowbird Act highlights a growing recognition that cross-border lifestyles are evolving. It does not yet provide a solution.

Until that changes, Snowbirds are best served by:

- Planning within current immigration limits
- Managing tax exposure proactively

- Maintaining Canadian residency deliberately
- Treating proposed legislation as context, not permission

Those who do this are well positioned to adapt if reform eventually occurs. Those who do not often discover that waiting creates constraints rather than relief.

Looking Ahead: The Next Chapter

Chapter Ten explains why more Snowbirds are being turned back at the U.S. border in 2025, even when they believe they are compliant. It outlines how CBP evaluates multi-year travel patterns, Canadian ties, work activity, and stated intent, and why vague or inconsistent answers now carry greater weight. The chapter also provides real-world denial scenarios and a practical checklist to prepare for a modern border interview. It concludes by explaining how accurate day tracking and deliberate planning support smoother crossings under current enforcement realities.

CHAPTER TEN
CROSSING THE LINE: WHY SNOWBIRDS ARE BEING TURNED BACK AT THE U.S. BORDER

In this chapter, you will learn:

- Why U.S. border enforcement has become more pattern-focused and less forgiving for Snowbirds
- The most common reasons Canadians are refused entry, even when they believe they are compliant
- How CBP officers assess intent, travel patterns, work activity, and residency ties
- Real-world denial scenarios that show how ordinary Snowbird behavior can trigger problems
- How to prepare for a modern border interview using clear, practical checklists
- How accurate day records and disciplined planning support smoother border crossings
- What Snowbirds can control in a tightening enforcement environment, and what they cannot

What Changed at the U.S. Border in 2025

For many Snowbirds, the shock was not that rules existed. It was that the rules they thought they understood were suddenly being applied differently.

Canadians who had crossed the border for decades without issue began reporting a new experience in late 2024 and into 2025. Secondary screening became more common. Questions became more detailed. In some cases, entry was refused outright, even for people who believed they had done everything "right."

This section explains what actually changed, and why long-time Snowbirds are now encountering a different border environment.

Reason 1: Border Decisions Are Now Pattern-Based, Not Visit-Based

Historically, many Snowbirds experienced border entry as a single-event decision. A CBP officer would ask a few questions, stamp a passport, and move on. That approach relied heavily on discretion and immediate context.

That is no longer the case.

In 2025, border decisions are increasingly driven by **patterns**, not isolated trips. Officers now assess travel history across multiple years rather than focusing only on the current visit.

What this means in practice:

- One compliant trip no longer outweighs a long-term pattern
- Repeated seasonal stays carry more weight than first-time visits
- Consistency is evaluated alongside duration

A Snowbird who has entered and exited regularly for years may now be reviewed more closely than someone visiting for the first time.

Reason 2: CBP Has Greater Access to Integrated Data

Another critical shift is visibility. Border officers are no longer working with partial information.

CBP systems now allow officers to review:

- Full historical entry and exit records
- Length and frequency of past stays
- Airline booking patterns
- Property ownership indicators
- Mailing address consistency
- IRS-related presence signals

This does not mean every data point is reviewed every time. It does mean that when something appears inconsistent, officers can see far more than they could even a few years ago.

The result is a lower tolerance for vague explanations.

Reason 3: Intent Is Being Interpreted Through Behavior

Snowbirds are often surprised to learn that intent is not determined by what you say, but by what your behavior suggests.

CBP officers are trained to assess whether a visitor appears to be:

- Visiting temporarily, or
- Living seasonally

This assessment is based on observable patterns rather than stated plans.

Examples that now trigger deeper questioning include:

- Spending more time in the U.S. than in Canada

- Returning year after year for similar extended periods
- Maintaining a U.S. residence while minimizing Canadian presence
- Being unable to clearly describe a return plan

None of these guarantees refusal. Together, they can change how a visit is interpreted.

A Familiar Pattern, a New Outcome

A Snowbird who has spent four to five months each winter in the same U.S. location for ten years may feel established and compliant. From the Snowbird's perspective, nothing has changed.

From the border's perspective, the pattern now looks settled.

In 2025, that difference in interpretation matters.

Why This Section Matters

Snowbirds are not being turned back because they suddenly became non-compliant. They are being questioned more closely because **enforcement now evaluates history, patterns, and signals collectively**.

Understanding this shift is essential before examining the specific reasons Snowbirds are being denied entry, which we will address next.

Why Canadians Are Being Turned Back at the U.S. Border in 2025

Snowbirds who are refused entry are rarely told a single, simple reason. In most cases, the decision results from a combination of signals that, taken together, suggest the visitor no longer fits the profile of a temporary entrant.

Below are the most common reasons Canadian Snowbirds are being denied entry in 2025, based on current border enforcement patterns.

Reason 1: Too Much Time in the United States

Time is no longer assessed in isolation. Border officers now evaluate **how much time you spend in the U.S. relative to Canada**, and how that pattern has developed over several years.

Common red flags include:

- Spending close to six months in the U.S. every year
- Entering shortly after the previous stay ended
- Having a multi-year pattern of long seasonal stays
- Being unable to clearly state how much time is spent in Canada annually

Even when each individual stay appears compliant, cumulative presence can suggest residence rather than visitation.

Reason 2: Travel Patterns That Suggest Intent to Reside

CBP officers are trained to assess intent, not just legality.

Patterns that raise concern include:

- Returning to the same U.S. location year after year for extended periods
- Referring to a U.S. property as "home"
- Keeping personal belongings in the U.S. between visits
- Indicating uncertainty about when you will return to Canada

Intent is inferred from behaviour. What feels like routine to a Snowbird may look like relocation to an officer.

Reason 3: Working While in the United States

This remains one of the fastest ways to trigger refusal.

Many Snowbirds underestimate how broadly "work" is defined under visitor status. Even unpaid or informal activity can create problems.

Examples that commonly lead to denial:

- Remote consulting for a Canadian company
- Managing a business online while in the U.S.
- Attending meetings or conducting calls related to income-producing activity
- Referring to work casually during questioning

Admitting to work, even unintentionally, can override every other compliant factor.

Reason 4: Weak or Unclear Canadian Ties

Residency is not assumed. It must be apparent.

Officers may question entry when Canadian ties appear diminished or poorly articulated.

Indicators include:

- No primary residence in Canada
- Lapsed provincial health coverage
- Minimal time spent in Canada annually
- Vehicles, mailing address, or daily life centered in the U.S.
- Difficulty explaining current ties to Canada

The burden is on the visitor to demonstrate ongoing connection.

Reason 5: Vague or Inconsistent Answers at the Border

How questions are answered matters as much as the facts themselves.

Responses that raise concern include:

- "I'm staying for a while."
- "We'll see how long we stay."
- "I'm semi-retired."
- "Just helping out a bit."

These answers introduce ambiguity. Ambiguity increases scrutiny.

Clear, specific, and consistent answers reduce risk.

When Several Small Issues Combine

Most refusals are not caused by a single violation.

A Snowbird who:

- Spends extended time in the U.S.
- Owns U.S. property
- Has no clear return date
- Mentions light work activity

may be refused even if none of those factors alone would have caused a problem.

In 2025, **patterns outweigh explanations**.

Real-World Border Denial Scenarios Snowbirds Are Facing in 2025

Border refusals rarely happen without warning signs. What surprises Snowbirds is not that rules are enforced, but how familiar their own situation looks once it is viewed through the lens of enforcement patterns.

The following scenarios reflect the types of situations being reported repeatedly in 2025. They are not extreme cases. They are ordinary Snowbird lives that crossed an invisible line.

Scenario 1: The Long-Time Property Owner

A retired couple from British Columbia had owned a condo in Palm Springs for over a decade. Each winter, they spent roughly five months in the U.S., returning to Canada in the spring.

From their perspective, nothing had changed.

At the border, the officer reviewed their travel history and noted:

- A consistent five-month stay every year
- Immediate return the following season
- Minimal time spent in Canada during the winter years

When asked about their plans, the couple referred to the condo as their "winter home" and could not provide a specific return date.

The issue was not ownership.

It was **pattern plus language plus duration**.

They were refused entry and advised that their travel history suggested residence rather than visitation.

Scenario 2: The Semi-Retired Consultant

A Snowbird from Ontario described himself as "mostly retired" but admitted to handling occasional consulting calls for former clients while wintering in Arizona.

He believed this was harmless. The income was Canadian. The clients were Canadian. The work was limited.

During questioning, the officer asked what he did for a living. He answered honestly, without realizing the implications.

That single admission reframed the entire visit.

Regardless of where income was earned, performing work while physically present in the U.S. violated visitor status. The Snowbird was refused entry and warned that future admissions could be affected.

Scenario 3: The RV-Based Travelers

A couple traveling by RV had sold their Canadian home and planned to spend winters moving between southern states. They maintained a Canadian mailing address through a family member but had no fixed residence.

At the border, they were unable to clearly explain:

- Where they primarily lived
- How long they planned to remain in the U.S.
- What ties they still had to Canada

The officer viewed the absence of a Canadian base as a significant issue. Without clear residency ties, their visit could not be classified as temporary.

They were denied entry.

What These Scenarios Have in Common

None of these Snowbirds intended to break rules. Each believed they were compliant.

What changed was how their situation appeared when evaluated collectively.

Across all three cases:

- Travel patterns were consistent over multiple years

- Canadian ties were weakened or poorly articulated
- Language at the border introduced ambiguity
- Behavior suggested something more permanent than a visit

These are the conditions under which refusals occur.

Why Scenarios Matter

Rules can feel abstract until they intersect with real life.

These examples demonstrate that enforcement is not focused on catching bad actors. It is focused on identifying patterns that no longer fit visitor status.

In the next section, we will shift from outcomes to prevention by examining **how Snowbirds can prepare for the border interview**, using clear checklist logic aligned with 2025 enforcement realities.

How to Prepare for a 2025 U.S. Border Interview

Border interviews in 2025 are more structured than many Snowbirds expect. Officers are not simply confirming eligibility. They are evaluating consistency, intent, and credibility.

Preparation does not mean rehearsing answers. It means ensuring that your situation can be explained clearly and supported if questioned.

The following checklist reflects what Snowbirds should be ready to demonstrate at the border.

A. Demonstrate Strong Canadian Ties

Canadian residency must be visible, not assumed.

Snowbirds should be able to reference:

- A primary residence in Canada
- A valid Canadian driver's license
- Provincial health coverage
- Canadian tax filings
- Ongoing personal or family connections

You may not be asked to present documents, but you should be able to describe these ties confidently and consistently.

B. Present a Clear Travel Plan

Vagueness creates concern.

Be prepared to state:

- Your intended length of stay
- Your return date or timeframe
- Where you will be staying during your visit

Answers like "for the winter" or "until it gets warm" invite follow-up questions. Specificity reduces scrutiny.

C. Avoid Any Reference to Work or Income-Producing Activity

Visitor status does not permit work of any kind.

This includes:

- Consulting or advisory work
- Remote management of a business
- Regular professional communications related to income
- Describing yourself as "semi-retired" if work continues

If you are not working while in the U.S., say so clearly. If you are, entry may be denied regardless of other factors.

D. Know Your Day Counts

Officers may not ask directly, but inconsistent answers about time spent in the U.S. can undermine credibility.

You should be able to explain:

- How long you typically stay each year
- How much time you spend in Canada
- Whether your travel pattern has changed

Accurate records strengthen your position if questions arise.

E. Avoid Residency Red Flags

Certain behaviors complicate entry even if no rules are technically broken.

These include:

- Moving household goods into the U.S.
- Registering vehicles in the U.S.
- Minimizing or downplaying your Canadian residence
- Indicating uncertainty about future plans

Border officers assess the total picture. Small signals add up.

Why This Checklist Matters

Most refusals could be avoided with better preparation and clearer presentation.

Snowbirds who understand what officers are evaluating are far less likely to create unintended concerns during questioning.

In the next section, we will examine **how tools like disciplined day tracking support border preparation**, and how Snowbirds can reduce risk long before they reach the inspection booth.

How the Snowbirds U.S. Day Tracker™ App Helps Prevent Border Problems

For many Snowbirds, border issues begin long before they reach the inspection booth. They start with uncertainty. Unclear day counts. Inconsistent explanations. A travel pattern that feels compliant but is hard to articulate under questioning.

Border officers respond to confidence backed by facts. That is where disciplined tracking becomes valuable.

The Snowbirds U.S. Day Tracker™ App is designed to help Snowbirds **know their numbers**, understand their patterns, and explain their situation clearly if questions arise.

What the App Is Designed to Do

The app does not automate border entry or replace discretion. Its role is practical and focused.

It allows Snowbirds to:

- Manually record U.S. entry and exit dates
- Maintain an accurate record of total U.S. days
- View multi-year travel patterns rather than isolated trips
- Reference consistent data when asked about travel history

Manual entry is intentional. Many Snowbirds limit mobile data usage in the U.S., and manual control ensures accuracy without relying on location tracking.

Why Accurate Day Records Matter at the Border

Border interviews often involve broad questions rather than calculations. Officers may ask:

- "How long do you usually stay?"
- "How much time do you spend in Canada each year?"
- "Has your travel pattern changed?"

Snowbirds who answer confidently and consistently reduce follow-up. Those who estimate or contradict themselves invite deeper review.

Having reliable records allows Snowbirds to:

- Answer questions without guessing
- Avoid overstating or understating time spent
- Maintain credibility during inspection

Supporting, Not Replacing, Good Judgment

The app does not determine admissibility. Border officers do.

What it provides is clarity. Snowbirds who understand their own travel history are better positioned to present themselves accurately and calmly.

When combined with:

- Strong Canadian ties
- Clear travel plans
- Appropriate visitor behavior

disciplined tracking supports smoother entry.

Prevention Happens Before the Border

Most refusals are not sudden. They are the result of patterns that develop quietly over time.

By reviewing travel history periodically, Snowbirds can:

- Recognize when stays are becoming longer or more consistent

- Adjust plans before patterns raise concern
- Maintain alignment between behavior and visitor status

Key Takeaway

Border issues are rarely caused by a single mistake. They emerge when uncertainty meets scrutiny.

The Snowbirds U.S. Day Tracker™ App helps reduce uncertainty by giving Snowbirds a clear, accurate view of their travel history, long before questions are asked.

In the next section, we will close the chapter by summarizing how Snowbirds can travel safely in the current enforcement environment and avoid unnecessary disruption.

Staying Compliant in a Tighter Border Environment

The border environment Canadians face in 2025 is not unpredictable. It is simply less forgiving of assumptions.

Snowbirds who understand this shift are better prepared to adapt. Those who continue to rely on outdated expectations often experience frustration because the system they remember is no longer the one they are entering.

What This Chapter Makes Clear

Entry refusals are rarely about a single rule. They result from patterns that suggest a visitor's lifestyle no longer fits temporary status.

Snowbirds who travel successfully tend to share a common approach:

- They understand how much time they spend in the U.S. and in Canada

- They maintain visible and defensible Canadian ties
- They present clear, consistent travel plans
- They avoid work or income-producing activity while in the U.S.
- They answer questions directly and without ambiguity

None of these steps require perfection. They require awareness.

Control What You Can

Snowbirds cannot control how border systems evolve, how data is integrated, or how enforcement priorities shift. What they can control is how their own behavior appears when evaluated collectively.

Preparation reduces stress. Clarity reduces scrutiny.

A Preventable Outcome

Most border problems are avoidable. They arise not from bad intentions, but from misalignment between lifestyle and visitor expectations.

Snowbirds who review their travel patterns periodically, maintain strong ties at home, and prepare for questioning reduce the likelihood of disruption significantly.

ABOUT THE AUTHOR

Gerald A. Scott was raised in a small coastal community on Vancouver Island, home to fewer than 2,000 people, where life moved at a slower pace and family time was valued. The fourth of five children, Gerald grew up in a hardworking family where independence was encouraged and shared experiences were enjoyed.

In 1983, Gerald moved to Vancouver on his own, beginning a chapter shaped by learning, persistence, and gradual direction. After navigating an unconventional early path, he found his way into financial services, eventually becoming a licensed portfolio manager in both Canada and the United States.

He later founded a firm focused on cross-border financial planning, helping Canadians moving south and Americans returning north navigate the financial, tax, and residency complexities of life across borders. Splitting his time between Canada and Maui, Gerald combines professional expertise with firsthand experience.

Gerald is the founder of the **Snowbirds U.S. Day Tracker™**, **Canada Physical Presence Tracker™**, and the **Snowbirds Expat Radio Podcast**, platforms designed to educate, inform, and simplify life for snowbirds and expatriates.

Outside of work, Gerald enjoys golf, mountain biking, reading, learning, problem-solving, and laughter. He believes in staying curious, maintaining perspective, and treating people with kindness and respect.

www.ingramcontent.com/pod-product-compliance
Lightning Source LLC
Chambersburg PA
CBHW060633080726
47818CB00003B/119